THE INNER SANCTUARY

THE INNER SANCTUARY

An Exposition of John 13–17

Charles Ross

THE BANNER OF TRUTH TRUST

THE BANNER OF TRUTH TRUST
3 Murrayfield Road, Edinburgh EH12 6EL
P.O. Box 621, Carlisle, PA 17013, USA

*

First published 1888
First Banner of Truth edition 1967
Reprinted 1992
Re-typeset edition 2016

ISBN
Print: 978 0 85151 042 2
EPUB: 978 1 84871 672 8
Kindle: 978 1 84871 673 5

*

Typeset in 10.5/14pt Sabon Oldstyle
at The Banner of Truth Trust, Edinburgh

Printed in the USA by
Versa Press Inc.,
East Peoria, IL

Contents

Preface

THIS volume contains the substance of several discourses preached to my congregation, in the spring and summer months of 1887. The subject is a very high and spiritual one; and I certainly feel as if I owed an apology for having undertaken to deal with it, at least in this form. But I have somewhat to say for myself. Most truly can I say that I have had great enjoyment in the private study of this portion of the divine word, as well as in the public exposition of it from the pulpit. Some of the manuscripts fell into the hands of kind friends, who were also very competent judges; the perusal of these discourses was followed with an earnest request that the whole series should appear in a permanent form; and rightly or wrongly, I have been induced, after much hesitation, to consent. But a Christian minister should regard it as a sufficient reason for appearing in the character of an author—at any rate, it ought to be sufficient for his own people—if he can truly say with Peter, and in somewhat of the same spirit: 'Moreover, I will endeavour that ye may be able after my decease to have these things always in remembrance.'

It will be seen at a glance that it would have been altogether inconsistent with the character and aim of a work written in such circumstances as I have indicated, to burden its pages with the names of critical authorities. Suffice it for me now to say that I have carefully consulted—besides the ordinary English commentaries—the works of Alford, Stier, Bengel, Godet, Luthardt, Meyer, and Brown. In perusing these works, notwithstanding their acknowledged excellencies often, one is painfully struck with the vast amount of conflicting opinion. On any difficult passage, scarcely any two can be found that exactly agree. While I have sought to make a legitimate use of these in making up my own mind as to the real meaning of the text, I have certainly called no man master. My simple object has been to ascertain, by means of the best helps, which God had put at my disposal, the mind of the Spirit for myself, and then to set it forth in as clear, and simple, and forcible a manner as I could.

In quitting the exposition of these chapters, a tinge of sadness and sorrow comes over me—to think what a glorious portion of divine truth has been gone over, and yet, alas! how little has been made of it. With the whole field of revelation before us, can we ever expect to find such a rich mine again? And yet it would be mere affectation on my part to conceal that I think I have indicated, with some measure of clearness, the successive lines of thought. In this connection, I would draw special attention to the Table of Contents prefixed as giving a brief sketch, at least, of 'the general lie of the country.' I may further state that my aim throughout has been to *suggest* thought rather than to *exhaust* any one topic.

And now, if I can only hope that this volume will be as useful to other hearts in the reading, as to mine in the writing, I shall consider myself amply rewarded for my labour. May the Comforter, the Spirit of truth, so frequently promised in these chapters, use this little book for the conversion of the unrenewed, and for the upbuilding and comfort of the body of Christ, and he shall have the glory!

CHARLES ROSS

25 April 1888

THE INSCRIPTION

John 13:1

Jesus Loving His Own that were in the World

John 13:1

THE narrative on which we are about to enter has always been regarded by true believers as a *unique* and most precious portion of the word of God. It is the record of the last moments spent by Jesus with his disciples before his passion. How was the Lord of glory employed? What was the work in which he was engaged during that solemn season? The beloved disciple, who leaned on his Master's breast, does not indeed narrate all that took place in the upper room, during that ever-memorable night—such, for example, as the institution of the Lord's Supper—but he does record incidents and utterances not mentioned by the other Evangelists, but of the most intensely interesting, instructive, and encouraging character, as revealing to us the Saviour's love and tenderness. The narrative as a whole may be said to comprise the three following things: First of all, the wonderful act of Christ washing the disciples' feet, with the warnings and indications, which he gave them in connection with it, as to the conduct of the traitor (13:2-30); secondly, the tender, consolatory discourse that ensued immediately after the traitor had left the supper-room (13:31-16:33); and then, thirdly, the sublime intercessory prayer just before entering the garden of Gethsemane (17:1-26). And the heading which John places on the forefront of the whole—not of the washing of the disciples' feet merely, but of this whole section of the Gospel narrative—the inscription which he writes on the doorway that leads you to the devout consideration of it is: 'Having loved his own that were in the world, he loved them unto the end.' All that Jesus now does and says, John traces up to love—pure, unmingled love.

I have often regarded this divine sentence: 'Having loved his own that were in the world, he loved them unto the end', as one of the most tender and touching in the whole word of God. The statement will appear all the more so, when viewed in the light of the context. For the inspired Evangelist not only specifies the precise date—'Before the feast of the passover'—but he also mentions a particular fact of a *moral* nature, of the utmost importance, as giving us an insight into the Saviour's mind: 'When Jesus knew'—or Jesus knowing—'that his hour was come that he should depart out of this world unto the Father,' etc. The idea plainly is that just *because* he knew—not merely *although*, but just *because* he knew—that his hour was come that he should leave this world, and that, consequently, his disciples would be left alone in it—as he had always previously loved them, so he now manifested his love in a very *peculiar manner, corresponding to their necessities*; and this, too, *under the most affecting circumstances, and to the utmost extent.*

In addressing you, therefore, a little more particularly from these words, I intend to notice, first, *the objects, the peculiar objects, of this love*, secondly, *some of those ways in which Jesus had always previously manifested his love to them*; and then, thirdly, *the steadfastness and unfailing faithfulness of this love under the most affecting circumstances—as in life so also in death*, 'He loved them unto the end'.

[1] The *objects* of this love are described, in the first instance, more generally as being '*his own*'. It is true, indeed, that in one sense all things are his own, as being their creator and preserver—all things, from the highest archangel to the meanest insect that crawls upon the ground. But his people are his own in a sense peculiar to themselves—his own in a sense in which others are not; his own, as given him by the Father, as purchased with his precious blood, and as being called by his Spirit; 'his own,' as being the members of his mystical body, and therefore standing in a nearer relation to him than angel or archangel. Oh, happy people, whom the Lord of glory regards as his own, his jewels, his peculiar treasure, his crown of rejoicing!

But the objects of this love are described not only as his own, but more particularly as his own *that were in the world.* Jesus had many of 'his own' that were now *in glory*; and doubtless these were objects of peculiar complacency and delight. Oh! see them in their white robes, as they shine so bright! Listen to their melodious songs! But still the precious truth for us is, that it was his own that were in *the world*, that he is here said to have loved. And why were they singled out from the rest? Why, but because of the *peculiar difficulties and dangers to which they were exposed*. Ask that tender-hearted mother which of her many children recurs oftenest to her memory—those of them who are safe at home under the parental roof, or the one that is far away at sea? And she will tell you, with tears in her eyes, that, while she loves them all, it is her sailor-boy who is exposed to so much danger. And just so, only in an unspeakably higher sense, while Jesus loves all his own, he regards with peculiar care, corresponding to their necessities, those of them that are still in the world. It is in this connection, that we see the full meaning of the *contrast* between his position and theirs. Jesus was now to depart *out of* the world, but they were to be left *in* it; and therefore his heart turned in love towards them.

And who can fail to recognise here, the close connection between the words of John and those of Christ himself in the intercessory prayer: 'And now I am no more in the world, but these are in the world, and I come to thee' (17:11). It is clear enough that the inspired Evangelist derives this part of his description from the words of his divine Master.

But without dwelling further on this idea here, is it not a most delightful and encouraging truth that, though Jesus is now in glory, yet he still regards his own that are in the world with peculiar care suited to their circumstances and necessities? Oh! think of this, you that go out and in amongst ungodly companions and that see and hear so many things that may well shock you if you have any spiritual life and tenderness. Jesus loves his own that are in the world still. But methinks, I hear some one say, 'Alas! I feel that I am in the world, not only because of the sins of others, but because I sin *myself*; because I have "a body of death" within me, and often it breaks out in word and action'. Yes, indeed, but Jesus loves his own that are in the world still; he sees and knows all the sin and imperfection that you have to contend against, and yet he loves his own notwithstanding. 'But, oh!' says some one, 'my case is of a different kind still: I have come hither today, burdened with a heavy heart'. It may be that it is some dear relative that is sick, and apparently near to death. All this proves that you are still in a world of sorrow. But then Jesus loves his own still and looks down upon them with ever watchful eye. This is the comfort of the Christian's heart and the balm of his sorrow; and I call upon his own to lay hold of it, to keep to it, and not to let Satan deprive you of it. Jesus loved his own that were in the world, while he was here on earth, and he loves his own that are in the world still, though he is now in heaven.

[2] But I come now, in the second place, to mention *some of those ways in which Jesus had always previously manifested his love to them*. For the sentence is so constructed and compacted as to imply that the Saviour's whole previous history had been one of love: 'Having loved his own that were in the world'—having always and previously loved them.

And here I might take occasion to speak somewhat of the great redeeming love of Christ to his own—those of them that were now in heaven, as well as those who were on earth—in undertaking our cause in the councils of peace; in the delight with which he looked forward, from all eternity, to the accomplishment of his work, 'rejoicing in the habitable parts of God's earth, and his delights with the children of men' (Prov. 8:30, 31); and in his appearing in the fullness of the times to discharge the great engagement (Psa. 40:11). But clearly the inspired Evangelist is speaking here of Christ's love to his own *that were then in the world, as distinct from that part of the one great family that had already gone home to glory*; and to this point, therefore, our attention must for the present be confined.

What, then, were some of those ways in which Jesus had *specially* manifested his love to his own *that were then in the world as distinct from those who had already gone home*? Indeed, his whole conduct towards them may be briefly summed up in these words: 'He loved them'. He always loved them; and there was not a single word that he ever spake to them, or a single action that he ever performed towards them, but it emanated from his love to them.

But more particularly here. See, for example, how, having once *chosen* them in his love, he ever afterwards proved his love by *continual companionship* with them. He sought no other company than theirs among the sons of men; unless it be that he often went to seek some strayed sheep, to bring it back into the fold. 'My beloved is mine, and I am his; he feedeth among the lilies.' *See, too, how tenderly, how graciously he instructed them.* His instructions were always *very simple*, because he loved them so well. They were exceedingly dull scholars, like you and me. There is no teacher on earth that would have borne with them as Jesus did; but their Lord and Master's love remained always the same; his love was stronger than their unbelief and ignorance. See, moreover, how ready he was *to sympathise with them, and to render them every kind of assistance.* Whenever they were in trouble, he was their willing and able Friend. When the sea roared and was tempestuous, and he slept, for a while, hard by the helm, they had only to awake him, and he rebuked the winds and the waves, and suddenly there was a great calm. When Peter's wife's mother lay sick of a fever, he did but enter the house, and speak the word, and immediately the fever left her. And when one of his dearest friends had passed beyond the ordinary bounds of life, and was not only dead, but had been four days buried, even then did he interpose, and prove that he was 'the resurrection and the life,' by crying, 'Lazarus, come forth.' Everywhere, and at all times, he was at the call of his disciples, ever ready to help them in every difficulty.

And, oh, with what *patience did he bear with them in all their weaknesses and infirmities*! On one or two occasions, indeed, certain of them were guilty of great impertinence. It was surely no small trial to the Redeemer's love, when Peter took him and began to rebuke him. What a sight—Peter rebuking his Master! Ah! surely thy Lord will have done with thee now, thou son of Jonas! But no, though he used a strong expression, to rebuke a temptation which was manifestly Satanic: 'Get thee behind me, Satan', yet his love to Peter remained unabated. Even when he rebuked him, he loved him. Oh yes, his love never faltered nor failed.

And who can tell in how many ways Jesus loves his own that are in the world still—visiting them with his gracious presence, instructing and guiding them by his word and Spirit, preserving them in his providence, strengthening them by his grace, comforting them with his love, and maturing them for his eternal glory?

[3] But what I wish you specially to notice now is *the steadfastness of this love—its unfailing and unflinching faithfulness, as in life so also in death*. 'He loved them unto the end'—not only to the end of life, but *to the utmost extent, and under the most affecting circumstances*. The meaning plainly is that as he had always previously loved them, so now, on the very verge of

his final sufferings, when it might be supposed that he would be wholly taken up with his own awful prospects, he was *even then*, so far from forgetting them that he scarcely seems ever to think of himself, save in connection with them. Herein is love, not only enduring unto the end, but moreover, most wondrously and conspicuously displayed, when, judging by a human standard, it was least to be expected. Oh, surpassing love of Jesus, with the fire of justice and the furnace of divine wrath, and the sea of his own blood—all, all in vivid array before him—he yet spends the last moments before his final sufferings in words and deeds of love to his disciples!

And if he thus loved them, in the view of the agonies of Gethsemane and the death of Calvary, think you does he *now* forget them—*now* that he has passed within the veil? Ah! no, it is impossible. He whose love the many waters of his own suffering could not quench, nor the floods drown (Song of Sol. 8:7), shall never cease to love his own that cling to him. And yet, what a wonderful truth is this, when we look at *what we are*! When we think of our sins and shortcomings—of our blackness, sinfulness, and vileness—what a wonder that his love is not exhausted! But no, the love of Christ to his own knows no change. It is a golden chain, without a single link amissing. Whom he has once set his heart upon, he will never cease to bless. And though we continually sin against him, and provoke him to jealousy, yet he loves his own still. For has he not said: 'For the mountains shall depart, and the hills be removed; but my kindness shall not depart from thee, neither shall the covenant of my peace be removed, saith the Lord that hath mercy on thee' (Isa. 54:10). And again, 'Can a woman forget her sucking child, that she should not have compassion on the son of her womb?' Can such a strange, unnatural thing as this happen? 'Yea, she may forget'—this strange thing may happen—'yet will not I forget thee.' Oh! how can he forget them? 'Behold, I have graven thee,' says he—not merely *stamped* thee, but '*graven* thee upon the palms of my hands: thy walls are continually before me' (Isa. 49:15, 16).

Oh! do not, therefore, child of God, get into the fainting fit of unbelief. For we have not to deal with a vacillating Saviour, who loves his people today and hates them tomorrow—a Saviour in whom I could have no confidence, and in whose existence I do not believe—but we have to deal with One who 'is the same yesterday, today, and for ever,' and who says: 'I am Jehovah, I change not; therefore, ye sons of Jacob are not consumed.'

But I must also add, if Jesus Christ loved his own unto the end, *then surely they ought to persevere in their love to him.* Sometimes we become greatly warmed up, and we do a great deal very zealously. But, alas! how soon we grow cold again. Let some peculiar trial or cross come, and we soon give way. Surely it ought not to be so. It was not thus the blessed Master dealt with us; he remembered us in the hour of his trial.

Oh, that his own love would constrain us to live upon him, and to live unto him!

But I have this also to say in closing, *what misery must it be to be without such a Saviour!* I scarcely know any words more terrible than these—to be without Christ. And yet I fear that, terrible as they are, they are applicable to some in this congregation. You have no interest in this heavenly friend, this mighty Saviour; your sins are still upon you: they are written down against you in the book of God's remembrance; and you will soon have to appear in his presence. But yet there is hope; for Jesus is the friend of publicans and sinners. Come to him, ye weary; welcome to him, ye heavy laden. Oh that you would come to him now, and then shall you be able to sing of unchangeable and undying love.

I

THE FEET-WASHING AND
THE TRAITOR REVEALED

John 13:2–30

Christ Washing the
Disciples' Feet

John 13:2–17

HAVING considered the general introduction to this subject, or the inscription on the doorway that leads to this whole scene, we come now to take up the several parts of the narrative in their order; and first of all, that which relates to the washing of the disciples' feet.

Of all the incidents in the life of Christ, this is certainly one of the most impressive and instructive. I do not wonder—whether I approve of it or not—that it has often been made a subject for the painter and the canvas; it is so interesting, so fascinating, and withal so fitted to impress our minds with a deep sense of the Redeemer's condescension.

The narrative contains, first, *a special preface or preamble* (verses 2, 3); secondly, *the strange act itself, with the conversation that took place when he came to Peter*—a most striking and instructive episode by the way, as it were; and then, thirdly, *our Lord's explanation of the act*. Let us attend to these three things in their order.

[1] First then we have here *a special preface or preamble*. I say *special* to distinguish it from that contained in verse 1. For, while the latter must be regarded as forming the preface, not to this chapter only, but to this whole section of the Gospel (13:1–17:26), it is perfectly clear from the structure of the sentence that this new introduction refers more particularly to this act of the washing of the disciples' feet.

And here again, as in the general introduction, the inspired Evangelist mentions certain particulars, which are fitted to throw light on this whole transaction. The first circumstance which he mentions is one of *time*: 'And supper being ended', or rather, being prepared, being made ready, for that it was not yet over is plain from verse 26, where it is described as still going on. The second circumstance relates to the *treachery of Judas*: 'The devil having already put into the heart of Judas Iscariot, Simon's son, to betray him'—referring to the agreement which he had already made with the chief priests (Luke 22:3–6). This circumstance appears to be mentioned here to show how everything was now hastening on to the great crisis.

But to these two particulars, the inspired Evangelist adds a third, *which affords us a glimpse into the inmost feelings of Jesus, and reveals the true character of the wondrous act itself*: 'Jesus knowing that the Father had given all things into his hands,' etc. This 'knowing' corresponds exactly with that of verse 1; and here, as there, the meaning is—not merely *although* he knew, but just *because* he knew—'That the Father had given all things into his hands, and that he was come from God, and went to God'. And who can fail to see here again, the close resemblance between these last words of John, 'That he was come from God, and went to God', and those of Christ himself to the disciples, 'I came forth from the Father, and am come into the world: again, I leave the world, and go to the Father' (16:28). Plainly enough, the Evangelist draws this part of his description from the words of his divine Master. But what I wish you specially to notice here is that it was just *as knowing all this, that Jesus proceeds to the menial service afterwards described*. In the full view of the power that was now to be put into his hands, and in the full consciousness of the glorious relation in which he stood to the Father, as having come from God, and as going to God—yea, just *because* he knew that all this power and glory belonged to him—he rises from supper, and begins to wash the disciples' feet. Oh, what wondrous condescension was this! Well might he say from his own example, 'He that is greatest among you, let him be as he that doth serve.'

[2] Let us, therefore, proceed to consider, secondly, and more especially, *the wonderful act itself, and the conversation that ensued when he came to Peter.*

How touchingly does the Evangelist set off the whole scene. There is such a beautiful simplicity, such a graphic minuteness in the description, as to bring up the whole picture before our minds. I think I see him in the very act of rising, laying aside his long loose robes, which would have hindered him in the operation, then taking a towel, and girding himself therewith—thus assuming a servant's dress—after that pouring water into a basin, and then proceeding to wash the disciples' feet, and to wipe them with the towel wherewith he was girded. I think I see him in the very act of washing and wiping. Everything is so minutely recorded. And no wonder; for everything connected with him is precious. And, besides enabling us to realise the scene the better, does it not give us a clear insight into the very heart of Jesus? Oh! mark, I beseech you, the calmness, the dignity, the order—I had almost said, the divine heartiness—with which Jesus goes about this strange work of his.

And what a *rebuke* to the proud and ambitious spirit that began at this time to display itself among the disciples! It is said that 'there was also a strife among them, which of them should be accounted the greatest' (Luke 22:24). And when we take the two narratives together, would it not seem as if our Lord intended—not only by his words, but also by his actions—to put an end to this spirit of strife and self-seeking? But however this may be, certainly nothing could be better fitted to humble the pride of man than the example that is here set before us. Oh, come and see this wondrous sight— the Lord of glory stooping down, and actually washing the disciples' feet! Is it not an amazing spectacle to which we are here introduced? Can we think of it without deep emotion? Can we fail to derive from it much spiritual instruction? He, into whose hands the Father had given all things, does, with these very hands, wash his disciples' feet! John the Baptist said that he was not worthy to unloose the latchet of his shoes; and yet he, of whom John thought so highly, deems himself not too high—not merely to unloose the shoes, but to wash the feet of his disciples! Let us put together the *thought* and the *work* of Jesus. His *thought* is, 'I am Lord of all; all power in heaven and on earth is given unto me'; and his *work* is that of a servant or slave; he does that which slaves only used to do; he washes his disciples' feet.

But what a scene when he comes to Peter! 'Then cometh he to Simon Peter' (verse 6); that is, in the act of going from one to the other, in the order in which they sat—the natural inference being that Peter was not sitting next to our Lord (verse 23). It would appear that our Lord had proceeded a certain length with this operation, without awakening any opposition on their part. But when he came to Peter, he immediately exclaims, 'Lord, dost thou wash my feet?' or rather, 'Lord, *thou my* feet dost wash.' It is impossible to express in our language the intensely vivid contrast between these two words, 'thou' and 'my', which, by bringing them together, the original sets forth, 'Lord, thou *my* feet—the feet of one so poor and unworthy. Ah! stop, Lord, would it not be more seemly that I should wash thy feet? Yes, Lord, and I would gladly do it; I would deem it an honour to be allowed to do this—to do anything for one I love so much.' And when you and I get such *an insight into the Saviour's glory*, and such *a deep sense of our own unworthiness as Peter had*, we too shall cherish similar sentiments.

Thus far, then, and in the question itself, I see nothing but the most profound and beautiful astonishment at an act of condescension which appeared to him quite incomprehensible. And accordingly you will observe that as yet our Lord administers no rebuke, but only bids him wait a little, and he shall understand it all: 'What I do thou knowest not now; but thou shalt know hereafter' (verse 7)—meaning presently; for indeed it was not long that he had to wait for an answer from his Master's lips (verses 12, 13). But viewed as a general principle, applicable to all dark sayings in God's word and mysterious dealings in God's providence, these words are full of comfort. Many parts of the divine procedure towards both individuals and the church of God at large, are very dark and mysterious to us. We cannot fathom the reason of them, nor can we perceive their end. But it is a blessed truth that this state of ignorance shall not last for ever. Sooner or later, light will be thrown on the dark parts of the divine procedure. The *future* will make it all plain. Sometimes, this revelation takes place in this world, after the lapse of a certain time; it may be a very brief interval, as in the case before us. But if time does not make all things plain, *eternity* will; there 'we shall no longer see through a glass darkly'; there 'we shall know, even as we are known.'

And now, surely, with such a promise as this, Peter will be perfectly satisfied. But no; but, instead of this, he says: 'Thou shalt never wash my feet'—more emphatically, 'never shalt thou wash my feet.' What obstinacy is this! It is impossible any longer to defend Peter; his conduct admits not of the least palliation or excuse; it amounts to positive rebellion. The element of pride and self-righteousness, which might have been secretly working in his heart before, is now fully developed, and stands forth undisguised. And yet how often may the believer be guilty of the same conduct still, spurning away from him the offers of the Saviour's grace. Ah! brethren, it is not true humility to *refuse* what the Saviour offers to do for us, or to *deny* what he may have already done for us, in his grace. No, this is not true humility, but pride—lofty self-presumption—not rare, however, in certain circles of lofty religious profession and traditional spirituality. The truest humility is reverentially to accept, and thankfully to acknowledge, all the blessings of his grace. Oh, let us take care lest, under the garb of a false humility, but really in the spirit of self-righteous pride, we be spurning away from us the tokens of the Saviour's love.

But our Lord is compassionate and tender, and therefore he does not take Peter at his word, but says, 'If I wash thee not, thou hast no part with me' (verse 8). What! If I wash thee not in water; nay, but if I wash thee not in my atoning blood. We have here just one of those instances in which our Lord makes a happy transition from the lower sphere of nature to the higher sphere of grace. In the fourth chapter of this Gospel, for example, he goes on, from the water in Jacob's well, to tell the woman of Samaria of the water of eternal life. In the sixth chapter again, we find him speaking to the Jews of the manna in the wilderness, and then, suddenly, he passes on to speak of himself as the Bread of God, which came down from heaven. And just so here, from the lower washing with water he passes on, because of Peter's resistance, to speak of his need of the higher washing in atoning blood. That it is of *spiritual* cleansing that our Lord is now speaking is obvious from the words, 'Ye are clean, but not all' (verse 10). What Peter could not submit to was that the Master should serve the servant. But our Lord would intimate to him that he had more to do for him than that; he had to wash him in atoning blood, or he could have no part with him. 'The Son of man came not to be ministered unto, but to minister, and to give his life a ransom for many.' And if Peter could not submit to let his Master go down so low as to wash his feet, how could he submit to be indebted to him for the shedding of his blood. Ah! brethren, Christ has infinitely more to do for us than to bestow any mere outward blessing.

And what is the *effect of this explanation upon Peter?* 'Lord, not my feet only', says he, 'but also my hands and my head.' Like thyself again, Peter! From one extreme to another. Formerly he said, 'Never shalt thou wash my feet'; but now, no sooner has he learned the true meaning of it, than he runs to the opposite extreme. And yet who can fail to see in these words *the strength and ardour of Peter's love to the Saviour?* 'Lord, to be separated from thee is death; and, if that be the meaning of my words, I am ashamed of them, I retract every word. And if to be washed has such spiritual significance, then not my feet only, but also my hands and my head.' Ah! yes, in this artless expression of life- and-death-like clinging to the Saviour, we behold the intensity and warmth of Peter's love. It just reminds us of his words on another occasion, 'Lord, to whom shall we go? Thou hast the words of eternal life.' And yet who can fail to see here also, Peter's *characteristic impetuosity?* Peter was always running to extremes. 'Never shalt thou wash my feet'—this was one extreme. 'Lord, not my feet only, but also my hands and my head'—this was the opposite extreme. Oh, what weak and imperfect creatures are we, even at our best estate!

But the Lord in his tenderness will correct this new mistake into which his servant has fallen: 'He that is washed needeth not save to wash his feet, but is clean every whit' (verse 10). We have here one of our Lord's most profound and instructive utterances. In our English version the word 'wash' is used twice; but in the original it is remarkable, that in the first branch of the sentence, our Lord introduces *an entirely different word from that which he had used before*, and which signifies to *wash all over, as in a bath*; whereas, in the latter part of the sentence, *the old word is retained*, which signifies only *to wash the hands or feet*. And the idea is that the soul that has been once washed, in the comprehensive sense of being born again, and of being justified, does not need in *that* sense to be washed again; but *only to be cleansed from the sins of his daily life and conversation*. Ah! it is a most significant and blessed truth that is here brought before us. When once a soul is truly born again and justified, he does *not* need to be born again and justified the *second* time. No, that is done *at once* and *for ever*, and, therefore, our Lord refuses to extend the cleansing all over, lest the symbolical instruction intended to be conveyed should be marred. But while the believer does not need to be regenerated or justified the second time, he *does* need to be cleansed from the sins of his daily walk—just as the man that has been in the bath, may need to have his feet cleansed from the defilement that he has contracted, in consequence of contact with the earth.

'And ye are clean', continues the Saviour; that is, in the great comprehensive sense, 'but not all'—referring, of course, to Judas—and a most important statement, as serving to show that, from the very first, there was a *radical difference* between him and the rest; and that, instead of being as true-hearted as the rest were at the first, and only falling away afterwards—as some would represent him—he had never experienced that *great spiritual cleansing*, which made the rest what they were. He had never been in the bath; his heart was never right with God. And if in our Lord's little band of apostles, if among the twelve there was one who was not clean, how much it becomes each one of us to say, 'Lord, is it I?'

[3] But our Lord proceeds now to give *the explanation of the act* (verses 12–17). 'So after he had washed their feet'— the feet of Judas, doubtless, as well as of the rest—'and had taken his garments and was set down again.' Oh! I think I see him again, after all was over, taking to him his garments, seating himself again among them, and then proceeding solemnly to put the question, 'Know ye what I have done unto you?'—its meaning and design. Our Lord had promised unto Peter, that what he knew not now, he would know hereafter (verse 7); and he now puts a question to them all, which is obviously intended to summon their attention to his own answer. Accordingly, proceeding to answer the question, he says, 'Ye call me Master,' or Teacher, 'and Lord'—learning of me in the one capacity, and serving and obeying me in the other. 'And ye say well,' says he, 'for so I am.' Oh, see here the conscious dignity with which this claim to divine superiority is made! Is not this wonderful, following as it does immediately after laying aside the garments of service? And then proceeding to apply and enforce the lesson, he adds, 'If I, then, your Lord and Master, have washed your feet'—the feet of my servants—'ye'—who are but fellow-servants under me—'ought also to wash one another's feet'—not

indeed in the cold, literal sense, profanely caricatured by popes and emperors, but in the higher, spiritual sense of deeds of love and humility rendered to one another. I will not, indeed, say, that it is never to be done even literally, if so be that our brethren need this service at our hands. In that case, we must not shrink from it, nor consider the hands too nice to engage in such a service (1 Tim. 5:10). But, on the other hand, it is perfectly certain that whosoever serves his brother in self-denying deeds of love and humility, is obeying the divine injunction of his Lord. It is not so much *what* we do, as *the spirit* in which it is done, that the Master looks to.

And then, just as if to explain the whole matter, he adds, 'For I have given you an example that ye should do as I have done unto you' (verse 15)—winding up the whole lesson with the words, 'If ye know these things, happy are ye if ye do them' (verse 17). It is well, indeed, to know these things; but the promise belongs to them that *do* them—a solemn warning, too, that even among real Christians, the doing of such things would come far short of the knowledge.

On the whole, we might learn from this subject many useful lessons. See here, in the first instance, *the amazing condescension of the Son of God*. But see also *our need of daily spiritual cleansing*. This was not indeed the primary lesson which our Lord intended to convey to his disciples on this occasion; it was only an episode, so to speak, by the way—the conduct of Peter being the occasion of drawing it forth. But he who brings light out of darkness, and good out of evil, over-ruled Peter's resistance for this end. What know we of spiritual cleansing in the blood? If we are strangers to it, we have neither part nor lot with Christ. Not that the believer needs to be justified twice; but, as he has much sin in him and around him, he needs to be daily cleansed from daily recurring sins. Further, let us learn here *the necessity of self-examination*; for if, even in the little company of the twelve, there was one whose heart was not right with God—if there was one of them who was a devil—how does it become each one of us to examine himself as in the sight of God! And, lastly, *the true friends of Jesus are here exhorted to follow his example in deeds of kindness, love, and humility towards one another.* 'Let this mind be in you which was also in Christ Jesus' (Phil. 2:5).

Warnings as to the Conduct of the Traitor—The Traitor Indicated—His Departure from the Supper Room

John 13:18–30

IT is an unspeakable blessedness that Jesus pronounces on those who walk in the ways of humility and love, when he says: 'If ye know these things, happy are ye if ye do them' (verse 17). But, alas! at the same table with him there was sitting one who had neither part nor lot in this matter: 'I speak not of you all' (verse 18). Not that there was any doubt or uncertainty as to the final salvation of 'his own'. On the contrary, he knew whom he had chosen. It is true, indeed, that the word 'chosen' sometimes signifies merely election to the apostolate (John 6:70); but, in this case, there is a clear distinction drawn throughout, between Judas, who was chosen only to the outward office, and the rest, who were chosen also to final salvation. Yes, 'the foundation of God standeth sure, having this seal, The Lord knoweth them that are his' (2 Tim. 2:19). 'But that the Scripture may be fulfilled'; that is to say, this has taken place, not by any accident or mistake, but that the Scripture may be fulfilled: 'He that eateth bread with me' (Psa. 41:9)—as one of my family, admitted to the nearest familiarity with me—'hath lifted up his heel against me'—has turned out to be mine enemy. To lift the heel is expressive of bitter enmity and malice. In the Psalm from which the quotation is made, the primary allusion is to the treachery of Ahithophel against David (2 Sam. 17); but this is just one of those instances in which the parallel between the type and the antitype is exceedingly striking; and our Lord would teach us, that just as in the case of David, so also in his own case, it was his own familiar friend that was to turn out his bitter and malicious foe. The eating of bread acquires a fearful significance, on the understanding that he partook of *the sacramental bread*; and, indeed, this is just one of those passages which lead me to believe, with many able interpreters, that Judas actually did partake of the Lord's Supper.

But however this may be, it is most interesting to notice that even what is here predicted of Judas, viz., that he was to lift up the heel against his Lord and Master, was to be over-ruled for good: 'Now I tell you before it come, that when it is come to pass ye may believe that I am he' (verse 19). The treachery of Judas was indeed a dark and mysterious dispensation; and if the disciples had not been forewarned of it, it might have proved a fearful stumbling-block to them. But the *fact* that it had been foreseen and predicted by their blessed Lord, would *afterwards* be a real ground of faith and comfort to them. This is what Jesus brings before them in the words: 'That when it is come to pass, ye may believe that I am he'—that is, all that I declared myself to be, and all that ye have believed me to be—your Lord and Master.

But oh! the *deep emotion* with which Jesus now approaches this painful subject: 'When Jesus had thus said, he was troubled in spirit,' etc. (verse 21). The words, 'When he had thus said,' connect this emotion with the preceding discourse, in which he had already twice referred to the treachery of Judas (verses 10 and 18); and thus they give us to understand the real cause of his trouble. Not the pain, which was so soon to rack his body, nor yet the agony, which was so soon to seize upon his holy soul—it was not this which occasioned the sorrow with which his spirit was now troubled, but it was the *sin*—the aggravated sin—of the traitor. The *peculiar character* of this emotion, and its deep intensity, are sufficiently clear from the language employed: 'He was troubled in *spirit*'—*not in soul* merely, but in spirit (cf. 11:33). It was not merely the feeling of wounded friendship nor yet pity for the traitor, but it was a kind of holy shrinking, on the part of his pure nature, from the dread character of this most Satanic crime.

But what is the force of the expression: 'And testified?' It seems to point out *the greater clearness and strength* with which he now declares the painful fact, as compared with the more general allusions, which he had previously made to it (verses 10 and 18). The disciples had failed, it would seem, to take up, at least fully, his meaning; he will, therefore, declare the same thing more distinctly and positively, and in terms which cannot be misunderstood; while, at the same time, the words that follow, 'Amen, amen,' denote *the solemnity and the divine authority of the awful fact*, 'One of you shall betray me.' Oh, with what startling effect must these words have fallen on the ears of the disciples! Accordingly, we now find them no longer doubting the fact, but looking in amazement at one another, 'doubting of whom he spake' (verse 22).

Various other details of a most interesting kind are brought out in the other gospels, as, for example, (1) that 'they were exceeding sorrowful' (Matt. 26:22); (2) that 'they began to enquire among themselves who it was that should do this thing' (Luke 22:23); and further (3) that 'they began to say unto him, one after another, Lord, is it I?' What a view have we here into the very heart of the disciples! Honest, guileless, simple-hearted men! they love their Lord and Master; they shrink back with horror from the terrible iniquity; but, instead of putting it on others, each one is most anxious to ascertain that it is not himself. Ah! it is greatly to be feared that some of us would be more anxious to put it upon others. But these honest-hearted men were more occupied with *themselves* than with *other people*; they had no time for hunting out the marks of insincerity in their fellow-disciples; they had enough to do with their own; while their putting the question at all was *the best evidence of their sincerity.* The Lord help us to imitate them in this respect! But, last of all (verse 24), we are told that Judas himself said, 'Master, is it I?' (Matt. 26:25)—feeling, no doubt, that, as all the rest were saying this, if he should be altogether silent, this of itself would be enough to bring down suspicion upon him; and therefore to prevent this the question is wrung from him. Or, perhaps amid the din and excitement of the moment, he uttered it in a half-suppressed tone or whisper, as I am certainly disposed to think the answer must have been, 'Thou hast said.' Or, possibly the indication may have been given to him by little more than a mere sign or token. At all events, it is certain from verses 28 and 29 of this chapter that up to the very moment of his departure from the supper room, he was not openly discovered, nor even suspected by the rest.

But, without dwelling any further on these particulars for the present, what an interesting and graphic picture have we presented to us in the verses that follow (23-26): 'Now there was leaning on Jesus' bosom one of his disciples, whom Jesus loved.' Thus modestly does our Evangelist refer to himself. It appears, however, from his words that John not only lay next to Jesus at the table, but that he also lay nearest to his heart. *'The disciple whom Jesus loved.'* The Lord indeed loved *all* 'his own'; but John was the object of *peculiar* love.

He, more than any other, resembles Mary, who sat at Jesus' feet, and heard his word (Luke 10:39). That he was the disciple whom Jesus loved—that he lay on Jesus' breast—this must have been the sweet solace of his heart; and on the Lord's breast, as the ancient fathers were wont to say, did he imbibe many of the heavenly truths and beautiful titles, which sparkle in his Gospel. Wouldst thou fain come near to Jesus, and even lie on his bosom? Then seek him diligently in John's Gospel, and, in company with the disciple whom Jesus loved, behold his glory—'the glory of the only begotten of the Father.'

But Peter, in his ardour, is anxious to ascertain who it could be of whom Jesus spake; and therefore, noticing the very favourable position in which his fellow-disciple is placed, he beckons to him somehow that he should ask who the traitor could be. And who will venture to deny that, in this request, Peter's passionate love to the Saviour does not conspicuously shine? And yet, when we reflect on what afterwards happened, it is certain that of all the disciples, he was the one most prone to think that he stood secure, and to plume himself upon his love.

But whatever may have been the state of Peter's mind, John takes the hint: 'He then lying on Jesus' breast'—or, rather, leaning over on Jesus' bosom—raising himself up still closer to Jesus, *softly* asks *in a whisper*, 'Lord, who is it?' And he, who of old had not been able to hide from Abraham his secrets, because

Abraham was his friend (Gen. 18:17), now whispers *inaudibly* into the ear of the disciple whom he loved, 'He it is to whom I shall give a sop, when I have dipped it'—a piece of bread soaked in the wine or sauce of the dish, and one of the ancient ways of showing friendship (Psa. 41:9). Having dipped the sop, he gave it to Judas Iscariot, the son of Simon. And thus the sign of Judas' treachery was, at the same time, *an expression of offered friendship*: it amounted to an offer of friendship at the last moment.

And yet, although the Lord's last act might seem enough to recall Judas, even at the last moment, still Satan enters into him. Most solemnising it is to read these brief hints as to the successive steps by which the traitor reached the climax of his guilt. The devil had already put it into his heart to betray the Lord (verse 2). *Wounded pride* (Matt. 26:14), *Satanic influence* (Luke 22:3), and *the love of money* (John 12:4-6)— these were the great evils that lay at the root of his conduct. And yet, who can tell what struggles he must have gone through, ere he brought himself to carry his resolution into effect? With the thirty pieces of silver already in his hand, he seems still to have trembled, and can we wonder? When Jesus stooped down to wash his feet, as I can have no doubt he did, who knows what compunctions he must have had? And as he listened to these solemn declarations of our blessed Lord, respecting one that should betray him, who can tell what dark thoughts must have passed through his heart? But step by step, he had opened his heart to Satan, until at last the die is cast, and his case becomes irrecoverable. Then came the terrible words, 'That thou doest, do quickly.' 'Thou hast done it already in thy heart; hell is already in thy bosom; why linger here any longer? Thy presence is a restraint; thou hast the wages of iniquity in thy hands, it only remains for thee to go and work for it.'

But before proceeding further with his narrative, the inspired Evangelist introduces here a *most important explanatory note*. 'Now no man at the table knew for what intent he spake this unto him,' etc. (verses 28, 29). From these words, we are certainly entitled to infer that, up to this moment, the other disciples were in ignorance as to who the traitor really was. If they had known that it was Judas that was to act this part, it is inconceivable that they could have failed to see the point of the Saviour's words as bearing upon his case. But no, not an idea of this kind seems to have entered into their minds, but they thought that, because Judas had the bag, Jesus meant 'that he should buy things that were needful for the feast, or, that he should give something to the poor.' It is clear, therefore, that they were still in ignorance as to who the traitor really was. No doubt it may be, and indeed has been, objected to this view that if Jesus had really given John to understand who the traitor was, he at least must have perceived the meaning of this saying. Certainly he did; nor is there anything to show that John does not *exclude* himself, while he is describing others. It is quite a common thing for a writer, while narrating an event of this kind, to exclude himself, and to speak of it only as it bears *on others*. But beyond these *two*—John, to whom the Saviour disclosed the secret, and Judas, who must have known what was passing through his own heart—it is perfectly manifest that, up to this moment, none of the other disciples knew who the traitor really was. Oh, it is amazing with what skill and dexterity Judas managed to conceal his whole character and plans!

But it only now remains that he should carry out his hellish purposes. 'He then having received the sop went immediately out' (verse 30). The whole affair must have taken place in the briefest possible time, since the words in verse 30 are connected immediately with those in verse 27—the intervening words being inserted by way of explanatory statement. 'He went out *immediately*'—thus separating himself, at once and for ever, from that holy society, with which he never had any spiritual connection or sympathy. And the last touch, which the inspired Evangelist gives to the picture, 'And it was night', serves to reproduce and to intensify the whole scene. This sentence, as well as the allusion to the crowing of the cock (verse 38), bind together the events of this whole narrative from chapter 13:1, and connect them with chapter 18:3. But I cannot help thinking that there is something deeply solemnising in this abrupt termination, 'And it was night.' But dark as was the sky overhead, there was yet a deeper, darker night in Judas' soul, and never shall one ray of heavenly light enter into it (John 9:4, 11:10).

Such, then, are some of the warnings and indications which our Lord gave them as to the presence and conduct of the traitor, and such the traitor's departure from the supper room. Let me now close this subject with a few practical reflections.

And, first of all, do we not see here *what a hateful, detestable thing hypocrisy, treachery is in the sight of God*? Oh see, only see, the Lord of glory troubled in spirit as he approaches the painful subject. And let us remember that hypocrisy is equally offensive to him still. Are we sure that there are no traitors of the Lord amongst ourselves? Judas betrayed his Lord and Master for 'thirty pieces of silver'—a very paltry sum indeed; but suppose that some tempting offer was made to you—that some thousands of pounds were put within your reach, on condition of betraying the Lord, his cause, his truth, or his people, into the hands of his enemies—are you sure that you would not make choice of the bribe in preference to Christ? Alas! it is greatly to be feared that Judas is not such a rare character after all. But let us never forget that no character can be more loathsome, more offensive in the sight of the holy Saviour.

Further, do we not see here *that sin, that hardness of heart is a gradual, a progressive thing*? Judas did not reach the climax of his guilt by a single leap, but step by step. It is said, that 'the path of the just is as the shining light, which shineth more and more unto the perfect day.' It is, indeed, a most solemn truth that a course of sin is also a progressive one, unless arrested by divine grace. Every time that sin is committed, it acquires new power over the soul; a habit of sin becomes a second nature, while, at the same time, Satan is ever ready at hand to second the resolutions of the flesh, until at last the measure of the sinner's iniquity is filled up. What, therefore, must be the fearful power of sin over the man that has lived in it, and practised it, for the last thirty, forty, or even perhaps sixty years! The Lord awaken such, ere yet it be too late, to a sense of their guilt and danger!

But still further, may we not learn from this narrative *that though the hypocrite and the hardened sinner may for a long time escape detection, yet at last he shall be disclosed.* The Lord may indeed, in his long-suffering, allow him to pass unknown, just to give him space and opportunity for repentance. And the sinner himself, on the other hand, may skilfully conceal his hypocrisy. But there is a time coming, when the hypocrite shall be unmasked, just as surely as Judas was at last. Sometimes this is effected in the present life, by prosperity or adversity. But whether in time or not, eternity shall disclose the deceiver, and present him in his true character. 'When the king came in to see the guests, he saw there a man who had not on the wedding garment' (Matt. 22:11–13).

And, *in the view of this solemn truth, does it not become each one of us to say for himself, 'Lord, is it*

I?' 'Search me, O God, and know my heart, and see if there be any wicked way in me, and lead me in the way everlasting.' 'Lord, thou knowest all things, thou knowest that I love thee.' Oh happy, thrice happy soul, that can, amid all its imperfections and weaknesses, with perfect integrity of heart, appeal to the all-seeing One, in the hope of being believed, because he knows his own work in the heart.

Finally, let the Lord's true-hearted ones *seek John's place—leaning on the Master's bosom.* What a contrast between John and Judas—John leaning on Jesus' breast, Judas proposing in his heart to betray him! Yea, what a contrast between Peter and Judas! For, with all the characteristic differences between John and Peter, sovereign, effectual grace, put an infinite difference between them *both* and their old companion Judas. Let us seek to have John's place. 'Nearer, my God, to thee!' Or, let us have Peter's place; but the Lord, in his infinite mercy, save us from the guilt and doom of the son of perdition! Not is there any other way of our being saved from it, than by a saving change of heart. 'Except a man be born again, he cannot see the kingdom of God.' 'Believe on the Lord Jesus Christ and thou shalt be saved.'

II

THE DISCOURSE AFTER THE TRAITOR HAD LEFT THE SUPPER ROOM

John 13:31–16:33

A Brief Outline
of the Discourse

IT would appear from the opening words of this remarkable passage that our Lord had spoken under a kind of painful restraint, so long as Judas was present among them. But now, on the departure of the traitor, all that is removed, and he pours forth his whole soul in one continuous stream, which only ceases as he is about to enter the garden of Gethsemane.

It is not, therefore, without good reason, that it has often been said that here we have 'The New Testament Inner Sanctuary'—its 'Most Holy Place'; within which Jesus holds the most loving and familiar intercourse with his disciples, *all of them now being 'his own'*. Oh, it is deeply affecting to notice how he now opens up to them, unreservedly, the whole secret of his heart, in so far as they were able to take it in. And most delightful it is, to trace the stream of heavenly truth and love from its rise to its close. First of all, after a most touching reference to his own departure out of the world, and their being left in it (verses 31–33), our blessed Lord proceeds to reply to certain questions put to him by his disciples—by Peter (verse 36), by Thomas (14:5), by Philip (verse 8), and by Jude (verse 22). These questions and their answers naturally turn upon the approaching separation, of which the Lord had just spoken to them, and which he now teaches them to regard as the condition of a speedy, a sure, and an eternal reunion. Then he concludes this part of the discourse with consolations and encouragements suited to the occasion. This extends to the thirty-first verse of the fourteenth chapter, which may be said to wind up this first part of the discourse.

But from this point, our Lord's instructions assume a somewhat different form; they partake more of the character of one continuous, sustained discourse—the disciples putting no questions—while Jesus takes a glance at their real condition and future career in the world. Then, again, he returns to the subject with which he had started—the approaching separation (16:16)—when the dialogue, or conversational form again appears (verses 18–29)—the disciples interjecting their remarks, and the Master referring to them, in the most loving and familiar way. Thus, like a dying father with his family gathered around him, Jesus begins this heavenly discourse, by speaking of his approaching departure; then their present condition and future career in the world are clearly set before them, and he tells them what they ought to be in it, and what they have a reason to expect from it. After which, returning to the original subject of his departure from them, he breathes from the very depths of his loving heart those last blessed words, in which he bids them a long farewell.

Such is the briefest outline of the holy scene, which is here opening up to our view. And, for the sake of convenience, the whole of this discourse may now be arranged under the three following heads: First, *temporary separation to be followed by an eternal reunion*; second, *the condition, duties, and prospects of the disciples in the world*; and then, thirdly, *the conclusion of the discourse*.

[A]

Temporary Separation
to be followed by an Eternal Reunion

John 13:31–14:31

Christ's Announcement of His Departure—Peter's Question Answered and His Self-Confidence Rebuked

John 13:31–38

IN entering on the consideration of the first of these, it is deeply interesting to notice the manner in which he refers to the subject of his own departure (verses 31, 32). Not a word is said here of the dread character of his own sufferings, although they are now immediately spreading out before him. He does not even name them, save by announcing, as with a shout of triumph, that the hour of his glory is come. And what is even more remarkable still, five different times, within just as many clauses, does he use the word 'glorify,' as if to his view the cross were just at that moment lighted up with a constellation of glories. 'Now is the Son of man glorified, and God is glorified in him,' etc. (verse 31). Let us endeavour to ascertain the meaning of these wonderful words.

'Now is the Son of man glorified.' He speaks in the present time, as if the thing were already past and done. When, therefore, Jesus says, 'Now is the Son of man glorified,' the glorifying spoken of is not the same as that mentioned in verse 32: 'He shall also glorify him in himself.' For there he is speaking of the *future* glory that was to be conferred upon him as the reward of his finished work; but here he is speaking of the *present* glory of the cross itself—the glory of his obedience and sufferings, by which, as he immediately explains, he glorified the Father. Yes, the *Son of man* was glorified, for it is as the *Son of man* that this glory was conferred upon him. But, adds the Saviour, 'And God is glorified in him'—as if the glory of each person had reached its climax in the cross. But how can God be said to be glorified in him? All his perfections shine forth and harmonise in his atoning work. For herein 'mercy and truth are met together, righteousness and peace have embraced each other.' Herein 'grace reigns through righteousness unto eternal life.' 'And if God be glorified in him, God shall also'—in return for this, and as the reward of this, the highest of all services ever rendered to him—'glorify him in himself.' In the intercessory prayer Jesus pleads, 'And now, O Father, glorify thou me with thine own self, with the glory which I had with thee before the world was' (17:5). And now by anticipation, Jesus declares that that glory was to be his. Thus the future was lighted up with the glory of the past. Thus the cross reflected a glory which was to be enjoyed in the future.

And this future was just nigh at hand: 'And shall *straightway*'—immediately—'glorify him', referring of course to his speedy resurrection and ascension to the right hand of God. Thus triumphantly does Jesus refer to his own departure out of the world.

But from the heights of his own glory, he now descends, in tender pity, to the case of the little children that were to be left struggling behind. 'Little children, yet a little while I am with you,' etc. (verse 33). This term of endearment, under which he addresses them, 'Little children,' is nowhere else used in the Gospels: it is only once employed by Paul (in Gal. 4:19); but it is appropriated by the beloved disciple himself, who not fewer than seven times employs it in his first Epistle. As used here by our Lord, it affectingly expresses his parental affection to 'his own' (Isa. 9:6), and, at the same time, their immature, weak, and helpless condition, now to be left in the world. For thus delicately does he refer to it: 'Yet a little while I am with you. Ye shall seek me'—feel the want of me. He knew that the hearts of these weak 'little children' were yet clinging to his visible presence, and therefore he wished to prepare them for the time when every such sensible consolation would be withdrawn. And, as he said unto the Jews on two different occasions (John 7:34, 8:21), so he now says to his little children, 'Whither I go ye cannot come'; but oh! in what a different sense, as we shall presently see.

Meanwhile he lays upon them a duty, but one so pleasant that it will also become their own happiness.

What, brethren, was the first command that Jesus gave to his disciples, just as he spake of leaving them? 'A new commandment I give unto you, that ye love one another.' Not certainly as if we were never commanded to love one another before; for surely it was included in the great law of love (Mark 12:31)—but the meaning is that it is now enforced by a *new example*. That this is the new thing about it is obvious from the following words: 'As I have loved you, that ye also love one another.' Christ's love to his people, in giving his life a ransom for them, was altogether a *new* thing; and consequently, as a model and standard for their love to one another, it was also new. Hence, too, it is said to be both new and old (1 John 2:7, 8). And, moreover, let it be remembered, this love does not apply to the whole human family in general, but only to believers as such— to all that bear the Saviour's image, and just *because* they bear it. But, continues the Saviour, 'By this shall all men know that ye are my disciples'—disciples belonging to me—'if ye have love one to another.' For to such love, men outside the circle of believers know that they are entire strangers. Alas! that there should be so little of it inside the circle. And, perhaps, there may be an allusion here to an ancient custom. We are told that each of the different sects amongst the Jews, at this time, had some particular tenet or practice to distinguish it; one took this, and another took that. 'Now,' says Jesus, 'I fix on this as the badge or mark of my followers—*mutual love*. Look at me, as contrasted with all other masters; I am distinguished from all others by my love to my disciples. And just in like manner, a love like this should distinguish my disciples from all other men. "By this shall all men know that ye are my disciples, if ye have love one to another."'

So much, then, for our Lord's address and commandment to the little children. But the words of Jesus respecting his own departure seem to have made a deep and powerful impression on the mind of Peter; and from the depths of his loving heart, he suddenly puts the question, 'Lord, whither goest thou?' (verse 36). And here I may again remark in general that from this point and onwards throughout the fourteenth chapter, our Lord replies to certain questions put to him by some of the disciples. There is, first of all, this question put to him by Peter himself (13:36–14:4); then, secondly, there is a question put to him by Thomas (14:5–7); there is another by Philip (verses 8–21); and lastly, there is another still by Jude or Judas (verse 22); and Jesus tenderly and lovingly replies to them all.

But at present we have only to deal with Peter's question. What especially struck the mind of the apostle in the preceding saying was that Jesus was now about to leave them. Peter's mind dwelt on that painful thought, and so, in his ardour, he utters the question, 'Lord, whither goes thou?'—having as yet scarcely a glimmering of light. Our Lord, in his reply, reaffirms the same truth that separation was inevitable, but, at this time, in words full of comfort: 'Whither I go, thou canst not follow me *now*, but thou shalt follow me *afterwards.*' Oh, how different is this from what he said to the Jews! To them it was only, 'Whither I go ye cannot come'; but to Peter it is, 'Thou canst not follow me *now*, but thou shalt follow me *afterwards.*' When our Lord says, 'Thou canst not follow me now,' what does he refer to? Does he refer to the work, which Peter had to accomplish by his apostolic ministry? No doubt Peter had much to do in this character for his divine Master. And then, besides, Peter himself was not yet quite prepared for heaven; there was much to be done *in* him as well as *by* him. But still, the whole subsequent history leads us to think of something of a different kind. 'Thou canst not follow me,' our Lord would say to him, 'in my great redeeming work; but thou shalt follow me, after it is over, to my eternal glory.' 'Thou shalt follow me afterwards.' And, perhaps, there is an allusion in these last words to the peculiar pathway by which Peter would enter into glory—through *the martyr's tribulation.*

But Peter will insist on his *now*: 'Why cannot I follow thee *now*?'—'I who walked towards thee upon the waters, I who ascended with thee the mount of transfiguration—Why cannot I follow thee now?' Oh! why art thou in such haste, thou son of Jonas? Thou art not yet made strong, through the outpouring of the Spirit at Pentecost! But certainly Peter is in haste; and not only so, but perceiving it was *death* that our Lord had in his view, as that which would separate them, he, in a vain, self-confident spirit, declares that he would lay down his life for his sake. Now, there can be no doubt that Peter honestly meant all this—that he sincerely believed that he could do all this. But oh! he manifested great ignorance of the state of his own heart, great self-confidence, and, I must add, a shameful disregard of the words of his Master. Jesus had said, 'Thou canst not follow me now;' but Peter defies this word of the Master, and, instead of praying to be helped, and guarded, and kept, he boastingly exclaims that he is ready to die for his sake. Nor was he alone in this self-confident spirit; for, as another Evangelist assures us, the other disciples will not be outdone by this valiant one, but they vie with each other in declaring, that they will 'rather die than deny' (Matt. 26:35). Oh, how Satan must have laughed, when he heard this boastful, self-confident spirit!

But our blessed Lord, who knows us better than we know ourselves, tells this self-confident disciple whither he is tending: 'Wilt thou lay down thy life for my sake?'— repeating Peter's own words. Doubtless there is in this repetition deep, though affectionate irony, which Peter himself would afterwards keenly feel, as he recalled the painful scene. And then our Lord solemnly adds: 'Amen, Amen, I say unto thee, the cock shall not crow till thou hast denied me thrice.' That is what thou shalt do, Peter!—and if thou wilt not now believe my words of tender warning, thou shalt afterwards know it, by bitter experience, and the sooner the better! And, in whatever way we may reconcile it with his subsequent conduct, this prediction of his denial appears to have made a profound impression upon the mind of the apostle; he seems, for the time, to have been overwhelmed by it, and from this moment, he did not again utter a single word during these discourses.

But here an interesting little question might be raised, Why does our Lord particularly refer to the crowing of the cock in predicting Peter's fall? Why does he not rather say, 'Before tomorrow's dawn'? The answer is that the cock, with its penetrating watch-cry, was commissioned by God to be a preacher of repentance to the fallen disciple; and we know that afterwards, when the Lord turned and looked upon Peter, he 'remembered the word of the Lord'—this very word—'and he went out and wept bitterly' (Luke 22:61, 62). Ah! yes, brethren, there was something deeply affecting in our Lord's whole treatment of this disciple during this night.

Such, then, is a simple exposition of this interesting passage. But now to apply it to ourselves. See here *the glories which encircle the cross of Christ*. To the Saviour's view it was lighted up with glory. It is glorious in itself; God is glorified in it, in the salvation of sinners; and it is the basis of all the glory which now encircles the Redeemer in heaven. No wonder though Paul said, 'God forbid that I should glory, save in the cross of Christ,' etc. Oh, brethren, study God in Christ, and study Christ in the cross. It reflects more vividly the glory of God than if ten thousand worlds were called into being at his fiat; it is also the foundation of all our hopes for eternity.

Let us learn here also that *the state of the church on earth is, in a certain sense, one of separation from the Master—a state of widowhood.* Jesus was to depart, and his disciples were to be left behind in the world. Nor could they follow him now. His work *for* them, *in* them, and *by* them, must be done first. And just so, his people are now in a state of widowhood in the world. But then, the separation is to be only for a time. His work for them is already past and finished, and when his work *in* them and *by* them is also ended, they shall follow him to the glory-land. They 'shall follow him afterwards'—in the hour of death, and when he shall come the second time, to release his bride from the scene of her humiliation, and to make her manifestly and eternally his own.

But meanwhile, let us *hear and obey his dying command*—his first and farewell charge to the 'little children', when he had them all alone in the upper room: 'A new commandment I give unto you, that ye love one another; as I have loved you, that ye also love one another.' 'By all my love to you, by all the tokens of my love to you in the past, and by all the still greater tokens of my love that your wondering eyes shall behold in the future, I command you to love one another; yes, to love one another as I have loved you.'

Lastly, let us be on our guard against *the danger of self-confidence.* Let us ask ourselves upon what our confidence is grounded. Satan has a quiver full of poisoned arrows. Do you know which is the most deadly?

It is trust, confidence in thyself; it is a vain, self-confident, boastful spirit. Oh! see that the enemy does not wound thee thereby. 'Be not high-minded, but fear.' 'Let him that thinketh he standeth, take heed lest he fall.'

The Many Mansions—For ever
with the Lord

John 14:1–3

THE words of Jesus seem to have produced a deep
impression on the minds of the disciples, and they
are in consequence very sad and dejected. We may
well suppose a brief pause to have intervened, during
which his words have been sinking deep into their
hearts, and now they are greatly perplexed and troubled on account of the sad things of which they have
just been hearing—Judas' treachery, Peter's denial, and,
far above all, the Lord's own departure from them. Oh!
what a sad and trying position for the church of God
to be placed in; and this, too, just in proportion to the
measure of their love to him! But if sad and trying their
position, as rich and seasonable the consolations here
afforded them. For mark you how he begins his con-
soling strains: 'Let not your heart be troubled.' And
what is the great antidote which he prescribes for their
heart-troubles? They are exhorted to confidence in
God and also in himself: 'Ye believe in God,' or rather,

'Believe in God, believe also in me'—both clauses being an exhortation or command. And it is very remarkable that, whereas in the first member of the sentence, the word *believe* is placed before the object—believe in God; in the latter clause, the *object* is placed before believe—'in me also believe'—as if to bring out more distinctly and prominently himself as an object of faith. But what a demand was this to make by one sitting with them at the same table! When our Lord thus associates himself with the Father, as an object of worship, does it not amount to making himself equal with God? (John 5:18); and would not the thought rise up anew to their minds, Then thou art God? Indeed, it is not the transfer of our trust *from* one object to another, but rather the *concentration of it* upon the incarnate Son as the daysman, the mediator between God and sinners.

But what are they to believe in him for? What is the great work that he is to do for them, and for the doing of which they are to put implicit confidence in him? They are to believe that he, in his oneness with the Father, is to bring them to eternal glory. For what else, and what less than this, can be the meaning of the words, 'In my Father's house are many mansions'? etc. (verses 2, 3). These words stand in the closest relation to the preceding context. Jesus said unto Peter, 'Whither I go thou canst not follow me now, but thou shalt follow me afterwards' (13:36); and now, seeing their distress, he extends and applies the same promise to them all.

What they are here exhorted to believe is that in the Father's house, to which he was going, there was room for them, as well as for him. Although he was now going to leave them, it was only to prepare a place for them, and soon he would come again, and fetch them home to be for ever with himself. This is what they are required to believe in him for; and this is how Jesus comforts their sorrowing hearts.

Now, in speaking to you more particularly from these words, let us notice, first, *the name* which Jesus gives to heaven, or the place to which he was going—'My Father's house'; secondly, *the declaration* which he makes regarding it—'In my Father's house are many mansions'; thirdly, *the reason* which he gives for his departure out of this world, and his going to the Father; and finally, *the promise* and *the prospect* which he holds out of his future return, to take them to be for ever with himself.

[1] First of all, let us notice *the name which Jesus gives to the place to which he was going*—'My Father's house.' Sweet and attractive view of heaven! And certainly, whatever else be implied in these words, they convey the idea that heaven is the *peculiar dwelling-place of God*. When I speak of my father's house, I mean the house in which he dwells, which is specially his own, and in which I may expect to find him at home. And, in like manner, when Jesus speaks of his Father's house, he means the house in which he peculiarly dwells, which is peculiarly his own, and in which

he gloriously manifests his presence, as he does not anywhere else. It is true, indeed, there is a sense in which God is *everywhere present*, yea, even *in hell*, in the exercise of his *punitive justice* and *power* (Psa. 139:8). There is a sense, too, in which he is *graciously* present with his own, as he is not with the rest of the world. 'This,' said the patriarch Jacob, with his head upon the stones for his pillow, 'this,' said he, 'is none other but the house of God, and this is the gate of heaven' (Gen. 28:17). 'A day in thy courts,' says the psalmist, 'is better than a thousand' (Psa. 84:10). But it is evident from this, as well as from many other passages of the divine word, that, while there is a sense in which God is *essentially* present everywhere, and a sense in which he is *graciously* present with his own as he is not with the rest of the world, yet there is also a *place*, *a local habitation*, in which he gloriously manifests his presence, as he does not even to his own, whilst they are here upon the earth. It is true, we know not within what portion of his dominions his glorious presence is thus to be enjoyed—it has not for wise purposes been revealed to us; but this we do know that wherever it is, 'The glory of the Lord doth lighten it, and the Lamb is the light thereof.' Where is Enoch now in his glorified body? Where is Elijah? Where, above all, is the man Christ Jesus himself in his glorified body? Wherever they are, there is the Father's house; there is his throne; there are his attendants; thence he issues his commands; and there his presence is gloriously felt and enjoyed, as it cannot be upon earth. Oh! what a *holy* place that must be in which Jehovah peculiarly, gloriously manifests his presence! Thither surely 'nothing that defileth shall enter.' And what a *happy* place too! 'In thy presence is fullness of joy; at thy right hand are pleasures for evermore' (Psa. 16:11). Oh, sweet and attractive view of heaven! 'My Father's house'—the home in which he gloriously resides, the home which sin and sorrow shall never enter, and where there shall be no separation and no death; but where God dwells in the character of a Father, and where his redeemed family shall one day be assembled with him.

[2] But observe, secondly, *the declaration which Jesus makes regarding it*—'In my Father's house are many mansions', or rather, *dwelling-places, permanent abodes, fixed, safe resting-places*. And how sweetly does this contrast with their present state on earth! 'This is not our rest.' 'Here we have no continuing city.' Here 'we are strangers and pilgrims, as all our fathers were.' But 'there remaineth a rest for the people of God'; 'there is a city, which hath foundations, whose builder and maker is God.'

But what meaneth this word '*many*'? Not a few merely, not even some, but '*many*'. The image appears to be derived from those vast oriental palaces, in which there is an abode, not only for the sovereign and the heir to the throne, but also for all the sons of the king, however numerous they might be. And just so, in the Father's house—in heaven—there is room, not only for the king's Son, but for all the royal family. The term 'many,' therefore, is not to be understood as referring to *different degrees of glory in heaven*; at least, that is not the idea here; but it refers solely to the *number* of the abodes. The idea certainly is that the Father's house is a very large place, and that in this vast edifice, there is room enough for all Christ's followers. Indeed, we are elsewhere expressly told that the company of the redeemed shall one day form 'a multitude which no man can number' (Rev. 7:9). And I confess to you, I like this idea; I like to think of heaven as a very large place, and of the company of the redeemed as forming an innumerable multitude. And I do so partly because just in proportion to the number of the redeemed will be, in one sense, *the joy of the Redeemer*, who will see in each one of them of the travail of his soul and be satisfied; and partly because in proportion to their number will be *the joy of the redeemed themselves*. Oh! methinks that if anything could mar the joy of the heavenly inhabitants—as certainly nothing ever can—it would be the thought that their number was small. But no, there can be no room for such a thought; for in the Father's house are many dwelling places, and every dwelling-place shall be full. But the question for each one of us is, Shall I occupy a place in this house of many mansions? When one of old put the question to the Saviour, 'Lord, are there few that shall be saved?' our Lord does not say, whether they are to be few or many, but he returns this pointed, practical answer, 'Strive'—agonise—'to enter in,' etc. (Luke 13:23, 24), as if he had said, What matters it to thee, whether they are few or many, if thou thyself art shut out! 'Agonise to enter in, for many shall seek to enter in, but shall not be able.'

Such, then, is the view which the Saviour gives us of the Father's house. It is a place of *many* mansions or abodes, and countless myriads shall participate in its blessedness and glory. And just as if to meet their doubting, desponding fears, he adds, 'If it were not so, I would have told you.' That is to say, 'If there were not many dwelling-places in my Father's house, I would have told you, I would not have concealed it from you, I would have forewarned you of it.' This last utterance is intended to beget entire trust and confidence. It is just as if he said, 'Ye may place implicit reliance on my word, that in the Father's house are many mansions.' But would not the question now come up to their minds, 'But how are we to reach those blessed abodes?' 'It is well indeed,' might they say, 'to be assured that the Father's house is a large, spacious place, but how are we ever to come to those blissful seats of rest?' Nor is it difficult to see how unbelief would have answered the question, 'He is about to leave us; we are to be left in the wilderness as sheep without a shepherd. Alas! we shall one day perish in the hand of our enemies.' Oh! brethren, have you never felt a feeling of hopelessness stealing across your mind, as you thought of the Father's house, and this just in proportion as you realised its glory? 'I,' might such an one exclaim, 'with a body of sin within me, and with innumerable enemies within and without, and each one stronger than myself—I occupy a place in the Father's house! how can you hold out such a prospect as this to me?' But oh, how sweetly does Jesus meet their case: 'I go to prepare a place for you. I not only tell you that heaven is a large and spacious place, but I go to secure your entrance thither.' And thus *the very thing on account of which they were sorrowful, turns out, as is so often the case, to be the cause of unspeakable joy.* Why were they sorrowful? Just because he told them that he was about to leave them. But 'I go,' says he, 'for the express purpose—on this very errand—of making your place in heaven sure to you.'

[3] Let us, therefore, proceed to consider, in the third place, *the reason which Jesus assigns for his departure out of this world, and his going to the Father.* And certainly, when he says, 'I go to prepare a place for you,' he refers, in the first instance, to *his atoning death*, as that which would open up the way to heaven. For the door of heaven was closed against every child of Adam; paradise was lost in the first Adam, until it was regained in the second. It is true, indeed, that many had entered heaven before Christ came in the flesh; but then it was, as it were, on credit, God the Father putting trust, if I may so put it, in the covenant engagements of his Son. But when Christ was manifested in the flesh, he, by his atoning death and sufferings, set wide open the pearly gates of the golden

city for all his followers. Is not this the very lesson which Jesus taught the two disciples on the way to Emmaus, when he said, 'Ought not Christ to have suffered these things, and to enter into his glory?' (Luke 24:26)—as if he had said, 'Ye were thinking of the glory first, but I tell you that the sufferings were the predicted gate of entrance into the glory.' And is not this the teaching of the apostle when he says, 'For it became him, for whom are all things, and by whom are all things, in bringing many sons unto glory, to make the captain of their salvation perfect through sufferings'? (Heb. 2:10). And, indeed, if we would obtain a glimpse of the real character and glory of the Father's house, we would do well to take our stand beside the cross. For if heaven is a place, the way to which is opened up by the death and sufferings of the Son of God, then what a heaven it must be! Or, when, at other times, the exceeding greatness and glory of the Father's house is apt to dazzle the vision, and stagger the faith of the child of God, still we would do well to take our stand by the cross. For is it anything more wonderful that the child of God should be exalted to heaven, than that the Son of God should have come down to earth? Is the glorious scene on the hill of Zion anything more wonderful than the awful scene on the hill of Calvary? Nay, but the wonder would be, if, after all that Jesus has done and suffered for his people, any of them should be found to come short of it. But no, short of it they cannot come. For, having finished the work given him to do, Jesus arose from the dead, ascended up on high, and there he now is, as our head and representative.

And this leads me to remark that when Jesus says, 'I go to prepare a place for you,' he means that he was going as *their forerunner to take possession of heaven in their room and stead*. 'Whither the forerunner is for us entered,' says the apostle (Heb. 6:20). And there he now is, at the right hand of God, not in his own name merely, but in in the name of all those given him by the Father. Just as the high priest entered into the holy place, bearing on his breastplate the names of the twelve tribes of Israel, so Jesus entered into the holy place, not made with hands, but into heaven *itself*, there to appear in the presence of God for us (Heb. 9:24). And if one of those, whom Jesus represented on the cross, but now represents on the throne, came short of eternal glory, where would be the glory of Jesus as the forerunner of his people? Every beam of it would be tarnished for ever.

But I cannot help remarking that there is not only an *outward preparation of the place for the people*, but also an *inward preparation of the people for the place*. *Heaven is a prepared place for a prepared people*, and the one is just as needful, in its own place, as the other. Who does not know that much of the happiness of an intelligent, moral agent, depends on the adaptation of his moral nature to the scene around him? It is so on this side of eternity, and we know that it must be so on the other. Jesus has gone to prepare a place for his people, and we know that it is such as to make them eternally happy. But what if the preparation should all end on the one side? We have no meetness, no fitness, no adaptation for heaven. On the contrary, we are 'vessels of wrath fitted for destruction.' Oh! have you never thought of what is said of Judas, 'He went to his own place'? Brief but most emphatic testimony!—'his own place'—the place for which he had been ripening—the place that was congenial to his depraved tastes and habits. And that is an epitaph that may be written on every tombstone in the churchyard, 'Here lies the dust of one who went to his own place.' But, blessed be God! it is a most precious truth that while Jesus is on high, preparing the place for the people, he at the same time *prepares the people for the place*. And how does he do it? He intercedes with the Father on their behalf: 'Sanctify them through thy truth, thy word is truth.' And he sends forth the quickening Spirit, by whose blessed agency they are renewed, sanctified, and made meet for the inheritance of the saints in light.

Let us beware, therefore, of attempting to separate between two things, which God has so closely joined together. The one, I repeat, is just as necessary, in its own place, as the other. And if any of you is disposed to put the question, How shall I know if Jesus is on high preparing a place for me? I reply by putting another question, Is he preparing you for the place? Are you born again? Are you growing in grace and in meetness for heaven? Oh, if not, you have no evidence as yet that he is on high for you. But, on the other hand, wherever there is true love to the Saviour, there you have an evidence, as clear as though the heavens above were to rend asunder, and you were to hear the voice of God, audibly addressed to you, that Jesus is on high for you. And soon he will come to take you to himself.

[4] In the fourth place, consider *the promise and the prospect which he holds out to them of his future return.* 'And if I go and prepare a place for you, I will come again and receive you unto myself,' etc. When our Lord says, 'If I go', we are not to understand this as if there were any *doubt* or *uncertainty* about his going away; on the contrary, he has already expressly declared, 'I go to prepare a place for you.' But it is just as if he had said, 'It is not more certain that I am now to leave you, than it is that I will come again.' And let us remember that, while there is a sense in which Jesus comes to his people in the power of his Spirit (verses 18–23), and also in the hour of death to fetch each of them away to be with himself (Phil. 1:23), yet the promise of the text is one which will not receive its full accomplishment until he comes the second time, to release his Bride from the scene of her humiliation, and to make her manifestly and eternally his own. That this is the full meaning is obvious from the words, 'And receive you *unto myself'*— unto sweeter, closer fellowship with myself—'that *where I am* there ye may be also' (17:24). Oh yes, he will never be fully satisfied until he has them all home

to be eternally with himself. And is not this the sweet-
est, the chiefest ingredient in heavenly happiness—*to be
for ever with the Lord*? (1 Thess. 4:17). How sweetly
therefore must these words have fallen on the ears of
the disciples! Why were they sorrowful? Because he told
them that he was just going to leave them. But, says he,
'It is not a final parting—it is not an eternal farewell.
I shall see you again, and your hearts shall rejoice.' 'Is
not this enough? Ye shall be eternally with myself in
my Father's house.' But what is this? What is this, 'to
be for ever with the Lord'—looking on his blessed face,
listening to his blessed voice, hushed to eternal rest in
his bosom, and casting down their crowns throughout
eternity at his feet! Pause, child of God; ere long it will
be yours—not by hearing, but in blessed experience.

But the ungodly, the unbelieving—the Christless, the
prayerless—ah! where are ye to spend your eternity? I
confess to you that, when I look into the faces of some
of my hearers, a feeling of unutterable sadness sometimes comes over me; for I fear that, because of your
unbelief, you may never enter into this blessed fellowship. Let me just sound a note of solemn warning in
your hearing, and I have done. Look at yonder point
in the distant ethereal heavens; in that point, see a dim
and undefined brightness just beginning to appear: it
grows brighter and brighter. The sun grows dark before
a brightness greater than his own. Legions of angels are
seen darting from pole to pole. At length, that light has
reached its destined place. Then, suddenly unfolding,

appears a great white throne; on that throne sits, starry-resplendent, the man Christ Jesus, in all the glories of his Godhead, and in all the beauties of his manhood. The judgment is set, the books are opened, the trial proceeds, the sentence is pronounced—on the one hand, 'Come, ye blessed of my Father;' but, on the other, 'Depart from me, ye cursed!' Oh, how terrible will these words be, as they proceed from the lips of Jesus! Whither shall the poor sinner flee, thus dismissed from his presence by the impartial Judge? 'Into everlasting fire prepared for the devil and his angels.' But yet his blessed invitation is, 'Come unto me'; Come, ye who are in the days of youth; come, ye whose heads are growing hoary in the service of sin; come, ye whose sins are of 'crimson dye and of scarlet colour'. Come unto *me*—'the rose of Sharon and the lily of the valleys'; come, *only* come, and if my grace, my glory, if I myself can make you happy, you shall be happy throughout eternity—come, and 'thou shalt be mine in the day when I shall make up my jewels'. The Lord incline and enable us so to do, 'and so shall we ever be with the Lord.'

Christ the Way, the Truth, and the Life

John 14:4–11

THERE is good reason to believe that the words with which Jesus winds up his reply to Peter's question, 'And whither I go ye know, and the way ye know' (verse 4), were intended to draw forth an expression of the doubts and difficulties, which he saw still lingering in their minds. Indeed, if their ignorance and uncertainty were to be removed, it was necessary that the thoughts of their hearts should be revealed. Wherefore our Lord often makes statements and puts questions that were fitted and intended to bring to the light the real state of their minds; and then afterwards he proceeds to deal with it, in his infinite wisdom and love, as the necessities of the case demand.

It was Thomas—doubting Thomas, as he has often been called—that on this occasion leads the way, as the exponent of their feelings; and the question that he puts is highly characteristic. He seems to be quite amazed at the Lord's loving declaration regarding them. 'Ah, Lord,' he would say, 'how canst thou speak so highly of thy poor disciples? No, alas! we know *not* whither thou goest, and *how* then can we know *the way*?' (verse 5). Thomas' estimate of himself and his fellow-disciples is just the *very opposite* of that expressed regarding them by their divine Master. What he has heard concerning the many mansions provided for many in the Father's house, and of Jesus' departure thither, to prepare a place for them, may have been the means of *whetting his desires*; but it certainly has *not* had the effect of removing his doubts and fears; and there can be no question that those doubts and fears were now a source of grief and sorrow to him, just in proportion to the intensity of his desire. Oh! it was *not* the *cold, painless* doubt of an unbelieving sinner, who is indifferent to the heavenly inheritance, but the *tormenting* doubt of a gracious soul that cannot make its way, through the clouds that envelop it, to some object on which the heart is set—it was this kind of doubt that Thomas here expresses. 'Would,' he would say, 'that we did know! but how can I give myself and my fellow-disciples credit for such knowledge as this?' And, whatever weakness and imperfection there may have been about him, the Lord of glory descried underneath it all an eagerness of spiritual desire. Such souls as these the Saviour always treats with peculiar tenderness. He esteems the dull disciple worthy of those sweet words, which have ever since blossomed in the hearts of all true Christians, as an unfading flower of the paradise of God. 'I am the way, the truth, and the life.'

It is an interesting and significant fact that whereas, in his reply to Peter's question, our Lord deals mainly with the *place* to which he was going, and their future reunion there, in his answer to the question put to him by Thomas, he deals mainly, if not exclusively, with the *way* that leads to it. And why? Peter is wholly taken up with our Lord's words as to his own departure. 'Lord, whither goest thou?' says he; and therefore our Lord directly answers that question, 'Whither I go thou canst not follow me now, but thou shalt follow me afterwards.' Thomas also is concerned about the 'whither'; but, in addition to this, he seems to be *specially* perplexed about the Saviour's words as to their knowing the *way*. 'Lord,' says he, 'we know not whither thou goest; and *how*—how is it *possible* that we can know the way?' And therefore to meet his case, our Lord proceeds to speak directly of the way: 'I am the way, the truth, and the life.'

Let us now endeavour to ascertain the meaning of these glorious words. The language certainly implies that the *old* way, by the covenant of works, is barred against us for ever. The door of heaven is shut against every child of Adam, on the ground of anything that he can now do or suffer. The glorious perfections of Jehovah—his holiness, his justice, and his truth—bar up the way; while, at the same time, the sinner's alienation and enmity of heart incapacitate and unfit him for entering thither. But the blessed news, which Jesus proclaims to us here is that he *himself* is the way. He has not only

opened up the way, but he is *himself* the way. Christ
in his person and work; Christ as the great High Priest
of his church; Christ as the mediator, the daysman
between God and sinners, is the way—'I myself am the
way.' So that if we would ever reach the end of which he
here speaks, we must have a personal interest in, and a
vital connection with, himself.

But the way—to whom or to what? The way to the
Father, for, says Jesus, 'No man cometh to *the Father*
but by me.' Instead of the Father's *house*, Jesus here substitutes the Father *himself*. For men do not first come to
heaven, and then afterwards find out God; but we are
first to find out God, and then come to heaven. Oh! let
us beware of imagining that we can be on the way to
heaven, while we may have no intercourse or fellowship, through Christ, with the God of heaven.

What a wonderful way to the Father is this! It is an
old way; for, in an important sense, he is 'the Lamb
slain from the foundation of the world.' Abel came
by this way to God, and so did all the Old Testament
saints; for, although redemption was not yet wrought
out, they were saved on the ground of the redemption
that was afterwards to be accomplished; they were
saved, if I may so express it, on credit, God having confidence in the covenant-engagements of his own Son.
It is a *new* way also (Heb. 10:20). The New Testament
church comes to God by this way; ay, and the church of
God will be eternally coming to him by this same way.
It is a way that shall never become old. It is a *living*

way, moreover. For Christ has eternal life in himself, and eternal life is the portion of all who take this way. And there is another thing in this connection, which ought greatly to commend it. It is a *safe* way; *none perish* that take this way to God: 'My sheep shall never perish, neither shall any man be able to pluck them out of my hand' (10:28). And, in a word, this is the *only* way to the Father: 'No man cometh to the Father but by me.' 'There is one God, and one mediator between God and men'; yea, one mediator, because there is but one God—'the man Christ Jesus' (1 Tim. 2:5). And this shuts out for ever all other ways by which men would seek to come to God.

But Christ is *not only the way to the Father—not merely this and nothing more; he is also 'the truth and the life.'* What is truth? It is God revealed. But Christ is the revealer of the Father, 'the image of the invisible God' (Col. 1:15); 'the brightness of the Father's glory, and the express image of his person' (Heb. 1:3). And what is life? It is God communicated to the soul, and imparting to it holy strength and perfect blessedness. But 'this is the true God and eternal life' (1 John 5:20). Thus is Christ 'the truth, and the life,' as well as the way to the Father. Not, indeed, that these three expressions—'the way, the truth, and the life'—are quite co-ordinate in this sentence; for most unquestionably the ruling idea is that of the way by which we approach the Father, as is obvious from the closing words: 'No man cometh unto the Father but by me.' Neither, on the other hand, do these three terms express a *single* idea—'the true way of life,' as some of the ancient fathers were wont to put it. But the meaning plainly is, that Christ is the way, the only way, to the Father; but the way, in such a glorious sense, that in him the Father is revealed, and in him also the Father is enjoyed; while, at the same time, the words, 'I am,' place the Saviour at an infinite distance from all mere creatures. A man can, at the best, but *show* the way to others; he can be neither 'the way, nor the truth, nor the life.' But Christ is *all* this in *himself*. Oh, what a glorious testimony in answer to Thomas' question! Christ, as the great High Priest of his church, as the mediator between God and sinners, is the only way to the Father; but he is so in such a sense that in him the Father is at the same time made known to us and enjoyed by us.

But, just as if to explain still more fully the truth that Christ is *the revealer of the Father*, it is added, 'If ye had known me, ye should have known my Father also' (verse 7). Not certainly, as if implying that there was any doubt or uncertainty as to their having known him, in some degree, before; for already he has said, 'And the way ye know.' But the *emphatic* idea here is the wonderful relation between Christ and the Father. So close is that relation that to have known Christ was to have known the Father. Let us see here, too, the consciousness of Jesus of his divine greatness and glory, of his perfect equality with the Father. But while it is here taken for granted, that, in a measure, they had known both him and the Father, yet Jesus points to a future, at no distant date, when they should know him more fully: 'And from henceforth ye know him and have seen him.' *'From henceforth'*, *including*, indeed, the present time, but embracing also *a future nigh at hand*. In fact, it was not until Pentecost that the double knowledge was fully possessed by them (verse 20).

But there seems again very good reason to believe that this last saying of Jesus, and especially the words, 'and have seen him,' were intended to elicit from them an honest expression of their feelings and desires. And accordingly you will observe that, while Thomas was now silent, that other disciple, who, a few days before, told Jesus of the enquiring Greeks—Philip—could no longer be silent, but must speak out the feelings which now arose in his mind: 'Show us the Father,' says he, 'and it sufficeth us.'

Here is a strange mixture of *nature* and *grace*, of *an earthly* and of *a heavenly mind*. Most unquestionably Philip believed in Jesus to the saving of his soul, and in his heart of hearts he desired to see God's face. Like Moses, he would say, 'Show me thy glory' (Exod. 33:18). But it is undeniable, on the other hand, that, in this request, there was much weakness and imperfection. For one thing, it is plain that he had practically forgotten, if he had not even denied, what our Lord had just affirmed concerning himself. 'If ye had known me, ye should have known my Father also.' To my mind, it seems pretty clear that Philip must have misunderstood the words of Jesus, 'and have seen him'—as referring to some outward vision or sign; and therefore when he cries, 'Show us the Father,' he means in some outward way, by some visible token or sign. A splendid vision—a magnificent appearance in the heavens—would be to him the best means of revealing the Father. It was just the very view-point occupied by those who demanded of our Lord a sign from heaven (2:18; 6:30), and which is still occupied by many, who are continually crying for signs and wonders before they will believe. And indeed, if the divine nature consisted solely in *power*, this request of Philip would have been well founded. But since God is holy and just, as well as almighty—since God is love—the true revelation of him could not be a mere outward sign; it must be *a living person*, manifesting in words and deeds *the very character of God*.

Wherefore our Lord thus tenderly and touchingly addresses this disciple, 'Have I been so long time with you, and yet hast thou not known me, Philip?'—mentioning him by his very name. 'What! have I been all this time with you, and yet hast thou—*thou, Philip*, one of my first and earliest disciples—not known me?' And yet how much more bitterly than over the blindness of Philip may he now bewail the blindness of many nominal Christians! To how many among ourselves might Jesus now say, 'Have I been so long time with you, and yet hast thou not known me, my people?'

And then to correct his mistake, Jesus plainly declares, 'He that hath seen me hath seen the Father'

(14:9; 12:45). What wonderful words are these to be used by one sitting with them at the same table! Where is the mere creature, either in heaven or on earth, that could adopt such language as this? The expression can only be understood on the supposition that he is a partaker of the same nature and essence with the Father. Not like Moses and Elijah does Christ reveal the true God; for when he shows the Father, he points not to one who is different from himself; rather is he himself the image of the invisible God. He who beholds a creature does not see in him the nature also of God. If Christ's nature were different from that of the Father, he could not have said, 'He that hath seen me hath seen the Father.' Let us, then, seek to keep Christ constantly before our mind's eye, as we would see God's face.

But further, our Lord *appeals to Philip's faith*, 'Believest thou not that I am in the Father, and the Father in me?' (verse 10). It is to *faith*, then, *not* to sight that the Father in him is revealed. When he says that he is in the Father, and the Father in him, he does not mean that he is one and the same *person* with the Father, for he often addresses him in prayer as 'thou' (chapter 17). The wonderful union of which he now speaks is that in virtue of which they live, the one in the other; or, in other words, it is that in virtue of which they are partakers of the same nature and essence: 'I and my Father are one.' Oh, never did the Lord of glory speak out more freely concerning his eternal Godhead—his perfect equality with the Father—than he does here.

And our Lord gives to Philip *two signs or proofs* by which he might recognise the presence of the Father in him—*his words* and *his works*. The first sign which he gives him is his words, 'The words that I speak unto you, I speak not of myself, but the Father that dwelleth in me;'—and now we would expect the words to run—he speaketh the words—but no, it is not so, but 'he *doeth the works*'—intimating to us that the works as well as the words of Jesus were revelations of the Father dwelling in him.

And now, on this twofold ground, he *demands faith* in this relation, in which he stood to the Father. 'Believe me,' says he; that is, 'believe me' *on the testimony which I give of myself*, 'that I am in the Father, and the Father in me;' while, in the latter clause, he points them to another ground of confidence, even his *own works*, 'or else believe me for the very works' sake'; by which works, Jesus evidently meant his *supernatural* works or *miracles*. These words plainly imply that his miracles were a ground of confidence, but, at the same time, a subordinate one, intended to support weak faith (10:37–8). In these words we have *the true position of miracles in apologetics, or as evidences of Christianity clearly defined*. These miracles occupy a real place as evidences, but only a secondary and a subordinate place, intended to aid weak faith. But without proceeding further for the present, let me now deduce some practical lessons from what we have already gone over.

And in the first place, what an insight does this passage give us into *the glorious all-sufficiency of Christ*! He is everything that the poor sinner needs. He is 'the way, the truth, and the life.' Are we shut out from the presence—from the favour and fellowship—of God? Then Christ is the only way of access. Have we lost the true knowledge of God? Christ is the glorious revealer of the Father. Are we destitute of spiritual life—shut up in spiritual death? Then Christ is our 'life'—all the life that shall ever flow to us and bless us, from the Godhead, thus approached and revealed. Happy, thrice happy, they that have an interest in such a glorious Saviour!

How interesting, too, to notice here *the characteristic differences that prevail among the children in the one family*! Already we have seen one of these children—Peter—so full of ardour and love, but withal so impetuous and self-sufficient that his Master had to forewarn him of his danger (13:36–38). But here we have another—Thomas—also so full of love and earnestness, but, at the same time, so weak, and timid, and doubting that he can scarcely give himself credit for anything; while there is still another—Philip—despite all his good qualities crying out for signs and wonders, while he ought to have been taken up wholly with his Master and his blessed words. We believe that we have similar differences among the children still; we have Peters full of love and zeal, but far too self-confident. We have doubting Thomases—Christians who are ever doubting *themselves*, but *not doubtful ones*; we dislike their doubts, but we have seen many doubters of *themselves*, whom we greatly loved. And we have Philips too—men who are constantly crying for marks and evidences of grace, while they ought to be exercising simple faith in Christ and his never-failing word.

But how wonderful does Jesus appear in the midst of his children, *solving all their difficulties by pointing them to himself*! He knows their inmost hearts; but he makes statements and puts questions that are fitted to stimulate enquiry, and to draw forth from them an honest expression of their difficulties; and then, having done so, he proceeds to take these difficulties out of the way at once and for ever. But whatever be the difficulty that perplexed them he finds the solution of it *in himself*. Does Thomas cry in his doubt and difficulty, 'Lord, we know not whither thou goest, and how can we know the way?'—Jesus says, 'I am the way, the truth, and the life.' Does Philip exclaim in his eagerness, 'Lord, show us the Father, and it sufficeth us'?—Jesus says, 'He that hath seen me hath seen the Father;' while, at the same time, he demonstrates the truth of it, by an appeal to his words and his works. Oh, let us rest assured that whatever our difficulty or perplexity may be, the proper answer to it is to be found in Christ, for he 'is all and in all.'

Jesus Answering Prayer, and Praying for the Comforter

John 14:12–17

IN the opening verse of this passage we have a very wonderful statement indeed, with reference to the believer. Jesus had been speaking of his own works—his miracles—as a secondary ground of faith. But he now declares in the most emphatic manner that they *themselves* would yet perform the very same; yea, greater works than these: 'Verily, verily, I say unto you, he that believeth on me, the works that I do shall he do also; and greater works than these shall he do; because I go unto the Father,' etc. The 'Amen, Amen,' with which the statement is introduced, announces the revelation of a new and most momentous truth. The expression, 'The works that I do shall he do also,' refers to those miracles like their Lord's, which were to be wrought by the apostles. For the works which Jesus did, his disciples also did, although always in his name and by his power. While the words that follow, 'And greater works than these shall he do,' refer to works of a *more spiritual* and *exalted* nature—such as were effected through the instrumentality of Peter, on the day of Pentecost; of Paul, all over the known world; and of any ordinary preacher of the word, when a soul is truly converted to God. Yes, brethren, the conversion of sinners to God is a greater work, in the reckoning of the Lord of glory, than mere bodily cures. It may not be of such a *strange* and *startling* character *outwardly*, but it is more wonderful in *its intrinsic nature*; it has a closer connection with *the glory of God*, and *the salvation of men*.

But does any one ask, How is this? How comes it about that the disciples were to work more wonderful works than those of the Master? Oh! it was not because of any might or power of their own, but because he was going to the Father. But what was there in this that was fitted to secure such a result? There, at the right hand of God, having reached the fullness of his power, the enthroned Redeemer answers the prayers of his people: 'And whatsoever ye shall ask in my name, that will I do,' etc. (verses 13, 14). But again, does anyone ask, Whence this prayer? What is the source of that prayer which Jesus delights to honour? It is thus explained by himself: 'And I will pray the Father, and he shall give you another Comforter,' etc. (verses 16, 17); so that the glory of these greater works is due entirely to himself. Let us, therefore, carefully consider this two-fold promise, or this two-fold explanation of these greater works, viz., Jesus answering prayer and praying for the Comforter.

[1] First, then, Jesus promises that from the throne of his glory he would answer the prayers of his people: 'And whatsoever ye shall ask in my name, that will I do.' Praying in the name of Jesus is here declared to be the disciples' part in these greater works. The believer asks, and the exalted Redeemer answers from the throne of his glory. It is not, however, to *any* or *every* kind of prayer that this promise is given, but to prayer offered up *in his own name*. But what is it to ask in the name of Jesus? To ask in the name of another is, in ordinary language, to ask as drawing upon his resources, and as if you were one with him. That other is supposed to have, by position or by service rendered, a right and title to what is asked; and he who asks in his name, does so, as being one with him, and as drawing on his resources. And, in like manner, to ask in the name of Jesus, is to ask as being one with him; it is to renounce all merit of your own; it is to ask as one depending entirely on his divine resources. And I need hardly say that prayer in the name of Jesus necessarily presupposes the Spirit of grace and supplication—the great pentecostal gift of which Jesus speaks at verse 16, and 16:23, 24, 26.

But who again is to answer the prayers of his people thus offered up in the name of Jesus? It is Christ himself. We should, perhaps, have thought that he would have said, 'That will the Father do.' But no, he takes it to himself, thus giving us clearly to understand that he is the almighty God, together with the Father. Oh, who does not see in this a ray of his divine glory? What a promise to make by one sitting familiarly with them at the same table! And all this, be it observed, 'that the Father may be glorified in the Son.' For the Son has no idea of setting up a kingdom of his own, separate from that of his Father, but disposes of all things, and over-rules all things, with a view to his Father's glory. His glorious motto is, 'Hallowed be thy name; thy kingdom come'!

Yea, our Lord *repeats* this glorious promise: 'If ye shall ask anything in my name I will do it' (verse 14). 'Yes, I say it again, you have only to ask, and I will do it.' By the word 'anything,' Jesus gives unlimited scope to the desires of his people. 'Anything,' that is to say, 'consistent with my glory and your own eternal well-being.' But beyond these two things, there is no limit put. It is an *unlimited* liability. We often see advertisements with the heading, 'limited liability.' But it is an unlimited responsibility on the part of Jesus! And, besides, he adds emphatically the word '*I*—I, who have never deceived you, and who shall be exalted to the place of infinite power—I *myself* engage to do it.' So close will be the connection, so intimate the communion effected by him between heaven and earth, that, while his disciples pray on earth in his name, he in heaven will act for them in the name and on behalf of his Father.

[2] So much, then, for the first promise here given. But our Lord next explains the *source* whence those prayers, which he delights to honour, really proceed (verses 15–17). As to the golden precept, which links the

two promises, 'If ye love me, keep my commandments,' it is clear, that we have here *the spiritual condition* which prepares the way for the promise of the Spirit. For, while the Spirit of God is the author of all that is truly lovely and good in the soul of man, there is an order in the bestowal of his gifts. First he gives one thing and then another. 'If ye love me,' says Jesus, 'then show your love by remaining in the way prescribed for you by my directions, and so you will be in a position to receive that supreme blessing—that blessing of paramount importance, which I now proclaim to you.' The commandments, to which he refers, are the orders which he had given them, and especially the instructions of that last night, regarding deeds of humility, love to one another, and continued confidence in him (13:13–14, 34; 14:1); while the connection seems clearly intended to teach us that *the fitting temple for the indwelling Spirit of Jesus is a heart filled with entire love to the Saviour.*

But observe very specially, that the *outward ground* or *efficient cause* of this divine gift is *his own intercession*, 'And I for my part will pray the Father, and he shall give you another Comforter.' His disciples indeed were to ask, but Jesus is also to pray the Father; and it is just *because* he does pray that the Spirit of grace and supplication is poured out on them. And here it is highly worthy of remark, that the word applied to Jesus is an entirely different one from that which is applied to his people, 'I will pray the Father.' It is a word which denotes *nearness, actual presence with the Father,* and so is employed to describe the mediatorial office of Christ in his exalted state. 'I will pray the Father,' as the man of his right hand. And what then? And 'he shall give you another Comforter.' In other passages Jesus himself is said to send the Comforter (15:26, 16:7), intimating to us that he had received this gift from the Father, as the reward of his finished work. But here it is, 'I will pray the Father, and he shall give you another Comforter'; and the lesson is, that the Spirit is the Father's gift to the church, through the intercession of the Son.

But *the title* which our Lord here gives to the Spirit—'another Comforter'—how deeply significant! The word which is translated 'Comforter,' literally means 'one called towards'—a Paraclete. The exact corresponding word in English is advocate—one who is called to defend, to interpose in behalf of an accused party before a court of justice. In this, its strict meaning, the title is applied by John in his first epistle (2:1) to our Lord himself: 'If any man sin, we have an advocate with the Father, Jesus Christ the righteous.' And indeed in this very passage, by the use of the word *'another'*, Jesus by implication attributes to himself also this title of Paraclete. In point of fact, what the Lord was to pray the Father for them was another to take up his place when he should leave them—one always to be within their reach, ever ready to come to their assistance in the hour of need, and that would never leave them, as Jesus was now to do in the body, but would abide with them for ever. And if I were now asked what this office involves, as descriptive of the Spirit's work in the church, I would say, it implies at least the three following things: (1) A helper to help them in their infirmities in prayer (Rom. 8:26); (2) a counsellor in the perplexities of life; and (3) a comforter in all their tribulations.

And thus, too, we see that the church of God has two Paracletes, or advocates—one in heaven with the Father, Christ, and the other on earth, in the heart of the believer, even the Holy Spirit. There is indeed a great difference between the work of the advocate within the veil, and that of the advocate within the church; but the work of both is needed for the salvation of the soul. Happy they who have two such glorious advocates to plead their cause—Christ in heaven, and the Spirit in the heart!

But just as if to explain still further who this Paraclete really is, he is also described as *the Spirit of truth* (verse 17; 15:26; 16:13)—not the true Spirit merely, but the Spirit of truth—the Spirit who is truth (1 John 5:6)—the Spirit from whom all truth proceeds, and who guides into all truth (16:13). Yes, he is the Spirit of truth *peculiarly and emphatically*. Teaching by the mere use of words can never give us but a very confused idea of divine things—the mere *image* of the things, and not the very things themselves; and this may be the reason why Jesus compares the instructions which he had hitherto given in this form to a mere proverb or parable (16:25).

But, on the other hand, the Spirit's teaching *causes divine truth to enter into the soul, gives it a reality within us, and makes it the very truth of God to us.* And if so, we may rest assured that this is no mere accidental huddling together of these two names. It is intended to teach us that there is a close connection between the work of the Paraclete and the truth which he communicates; in other words, he does the work of the Paraclete by applying the truth to the heart.

But, alas! for the unbelieving world. 'Whom the world cannot receive,' says the divine Redeemer. Ah, brethren, the world needs him much, for it is lying in wickedness and perishing in ignorance, and he is the only Being in the universe that can raise it up. But the world, in its present state, will have nothing to do with the Comforter, the Spirit of truth. And why? 'Because it seeth him not, neither knoweth him.' It recognises him not in his operations outwardly, nor does it know him inwardly, from its own experience; and therefore it cannot receive him. What the world needs is to be convinced of sin, of righteousness, and of judgment first; it needs to be converted to God; and until this is done, it cannot welcome him as the Comforter. Ah! brethren, it was by no arbitrary appointment that the Spirit came down first upon the one hundred and twenty only, on the day of Pentecost, and not on all the inhabitants of Jerusalem; the reason was that the former had received the one indispensable qualification to receive and welcome him as the Comforter; whereas the latter had need first to be convinced of sin and converted to God.

But over against this picture of the unbelieving world, the Lord in the most affectionate way places his disciples who can receive him: 'But ye know him'— already, and as opposed to the men of the world. And how? 'For he dwelleth with you.' Our acquaintance with him must begin *within*. It is an *inward* experience of his grace and power that makes men acquainted with the Holy Spirit. And while it is plainly implied in the use of the present tense that they had already the germ of that great blessing, yet it is clear that the fullness of the blessing—the closer relation into which he would enter with them—was still in store for them at Pentecost—'and shall be in you.'

Such, then, is the second great promise or explanation which our Lord here gives. And the *order* in which these things are fulfilled seems to be as follows: (1) Jesus prays the Father, who (2) sends another Comforter, who is also the Spirit of grace and supplication; then (3) the prayer of faith ascends in the name of Jesus, who (4) answers prayers by pouring out his Spirit in his quickening power, and by whose blessed agency these 'greater works are done.'

But before I leave this second promise, let me deduce from it, in conclusion, some practical lessons.

First, do we not see here *the divine personality of the Holy Spirit*? And I advert to this, lest any of you should take up the strange, half-sceptical notion, that the Spirit is nothing more than a divine attribute, or influence. Let any man of common sense read this passage, and he must see, I think, that the Holy Spirit must be a person as truly as Christ himself. Jesus does not promise his disciples comfort merely, but the Comforter. He does not speak of truth merely, but of 'the Spirit of truth'—*personal* titles. And if this is not enough, turn to subsequent passages, where he is said to 'teach,' to 'testify' (14:26; 15:26); and to the sixteenth chapter, where he is said to 'come', to 'reprove,' to 'hear,' to 'speak,' to 'receive'—all *personal acts*, and involving a real personal existence. Yes, brethren, the Holy Spirit is a *divine* person. For, mark you, our Lord's object is to comfort his disciples in an hour of peculiar sorrow, when he was just going to leave them; and what he tells them with this object in view is that when he is gone he will pray the Father to send them 'another Comforter.' Surely he considers this other Comforter quite *equal* to himself; nay, he tells them in the sixteenth chapter, that they will gain by the exchange. So clear, then, is it that the Holy Spirit is a person, and a divine person, equal with the Father and the Son.

How precious, too, to behold here *the three persons of the Godhead engaged and combining in the great work of our salvation*—the Son praying for the Spirit for us; the Father giving the Spirit to us; and the Holy Spirit coming to us—all telling us that God is well-pleased to bless his people, and to bless them with the full power of his nature.

But behold here also *a great test of Christian character*. I am not speaking to you here about a trifling matter. Our Lord draws here a broad line of demarcation between his disciples and all other men. And what is it? It is simply this: his disciples know the Holy Spirit; they know him from their own experience of his gracious work; others do not. His disciples have received the Holy Spirit; others have not. Are you a Christian indeed? Then the Holy Spirit is within your heart—working and dwelling there. Are you ignorant of the Holy Spirit—unacquainted with his life-giving power? Then read this scripture, and draw from it your own conclusion. You are still of the world, and what you need is to have your false peace disturbed, and to be converted to God.

Lastly, let us see here *the security and the ground of the perpetuity of the church of God*: 'Because he dwelleth with you and shall be in you.' Up to the present hour has this promise been fulfilled; and as it has been in the past, so shall it be in the future. Oh, what rubbish do men talk in these days about the safety of the church of God! But the two-fold promise, 'Lo, I am with you alway, even unto the end of the world,' and again, 'He shall be in you,' is a guarantee to the church of God that she shall abide for ever, and that the very 'gates of hell shall not prevail against her.'

Christ Coming in the Spirit

John 14:18–24

THE word which is here translated 'comfortless' is, literally rendered, 'orphans.' The expression contains an allusion to the title, which he had previously given them, 'little children' (13:33). But what wonderful words for a father to use, in the prospect of removal by death! No mere earthly parent, in a dying hour, could address such language to his disconsolate children; for indeed he must leave them 'orphans;' he cannot come back to them, but they must go to him. And yet Jesus, in the immediate prospect of death, could say to his 'little children,' 'I will not leave you "orphans." I will come to you,' or rather, 'I come,' or 'am coming to you.'

And if I were asked, What coming is it to which Jesus here points? I would unhesitatingly reply that it is to his coming *by the Spirit*, since it was to make his departure to be no *bereavement*. It is true, indeed, that Jesus came again to them, in a sense, when he appeared to his disciples after his resurrection. And it is also true that he shall yet come in a glorious manner, when he 'shall appear the second time without sin unto salvation' (Heb. 9:28). But it is perfectly clear that it is only of his coming in *the Spirit* that it could be affirmed that it would prevent their being 'orphans' in the world.

But what seems to me to place this view beyond the possibility of dispute is the connection in which the words stand. Jesus has been speaking of the 'Comforter, the Paraclete, even the Spirit of truth'—whom the Father was to send in his name; and then, without a single break in the connection—without anything whatsoever to indicate that he has changed the subject—he adds in the words before us: 'I will not leave you orphans: I am coming to you.' Does not this plainly intimate that the coming of which he speaks is coming in *the Spirit*? And the same thing is equally dear from the subsequent context. Those who apply this promise to the appearances of Jesus after his resurrection will find it impossible to reconcile this view with verses 20, 21, 23; for it is undeniable that these words found their accomplishment only after the outpouring of his Spirit on the day of Pentecost. And those, on the other hand, who apply this promise to his second coming, will find it equally difficult to explain verse 19; for there it is said that the world sees him no more; whereas of his final coming it is written that 'every eye shall see him, even they who pierced him.'

It is clear then—clear as a sunbeam—that our Lord is speaking here, not of his appearing to his disciples after his resurrection, nor yet of his second coming at the end of the world, but of something *intermediate*— of his coming in *the presence and power of the divine Spirit*. No doubt it may be here said that the Spirit is another—a different person from Jesus; but then let us remember that whenever and wherever the Spirit comes, *he brings Jesus with him*. Oh yes, he brings Jesus with him; it is not as a cold, indifferent guardian, or protector merely, of fatherless children that the Spirit comes, but as the blessed Comforter, whose work it is to glorify Jesus, to present him to the eye of faith, and to endear him to their hearts. Yet this much must and ought to be here admitted, that Christ's coming at the resurrection prepared the way for his coming in the Spirit, even as his coming in the Spirit prepares his people for his coming in glory.

Let us now examine this passage in the light of these general remarks, and we shall find it to be full of heavenly instruction,

First of all, our Lord draws *a vivid contrast between the state of the world in a little while and that of his disciples*: 'Yet a little while and the world seeth me no more, but ye see me.' It is just as if he had said, 'The world seeth me now, but in a little while, after my departure, I shall be beyond the sight of the blind world'—his bodily presence being the only sight of him, which the world ever had, or was capable of having. But in bright and blessed contrast to these he adds: 'But ye see me,' that is, with the eye of faith. For by the Spirit's teaching, Christ though ascended was to be visible to the spiritual eye. It is the same view of the glorified Saviour to which Paul refers when he says: 'Beholding as in a glass the glory of the Lord, we are changed into the same image from glory to glory, even as by the Spirit of the Lord' (2 Cor. 3:18). In short, while he was to be invisible, after his departure, to *the eye of sense*, he was from that time to be visible to his disciples after *a spiritual manner*. Well, therefore, does it become each of us to inquire, What do I know of faith's view of Christ as now ascended to the right hand of God?

This believing view of the glorified Saviour *is the means of all the Christian's life and activity in his conflict with sin and with the world*. For what else, and what less than this, can be the meaning in this connection of the words, 'Because I live, ye shall live also'? Take it simply and briefly thus: Christ lives; he is not only the living one possessed of essential life as the eternal Son of God, but he is also the *source* of life unto his people, as the God-man-mediator. But the question is, how is this life to become theirs? They behold him by faith; enlightened by the Spirit of God they behold him who is their life. And just because they do, the very life that is in Jesus flows forth into their souls. 'Because I live, ye shall live also.' In any case, Jesus, by the use of these words, 'I come; I live,' in the present time, transports himself in thought to that approaching hour, when, death being finally vanquished, he will live the perfect and imperishable life as the head of his people.

And from that time, being beheld by them in the light of the Spirit, his life becomes theirs. How secure, how blessed are they whose life is thus bound up with that of Jesus!

But our Lord proceeds to speak now of *the enlightenment to which they should attain as the result of the outpouring of the Holy Spirit*: 'At that day ye shall know that I am in my Father, and ye in me, and I in you' (verse 20). The expression, 'At that day', points to a definite time. All the events of his public ministry were connected with Jewish festivals. The feast of the Passover was to be the great period of his death; and as the time of this illumination was closely to follow that event—'yet a little while'—there can be no reason why we should not believe that the day of which he here speaks was primarily the day of Pentecost. And what our Lord affirms is that when that day should come they would then attain to a clearer perception of some most important truths than they had ever done before. The object of this knowledge will be two-fold—first, the union of Jesus with the Father, and then their own relation to Jesus. The first truth mentioned is the relation of Jesus to the Father. They had manifested considerable difficulty in forming a right conception of the Master's relation, as evinced by Philip's question (verses 8–10). But when 'that day' should arrive—the day of the Spirit's coming—they should understand it more clearly than they had ever done before. But the Master's relation to the Father was not the only truth on which the Spirit's teaching was to give them clearer light; they would then know better, also, their own relation to him: 'And ye in me, and I in you;' they would then feel that they were living in him and he in them.

And then *the process*—the successive steps—by which they should rise to this illumination are traced in detail (verse 21). Jesus had previously said, 'If ye love me, keep my commandments, and I will pray the Father' (verse 15, 16), but here he minutely specifies each link in the chain: 'He that hath my commandments and keepeth them, he it is that loveth me, and he that loveth me shall be loved of my Father, and I will love him and manifest myself to him.' (1) In the first instance, 'He that hath my commandments and keepeth them, he it is that loveth me.' This is he that is entitled to the special character of being a lover of Jesus. But (2) secondly, 'He that loveth me,' says Jesus, 'shall be loved of my Father;' for the Father loves all who love the Son, the supreme object of his love. And the Father loves them now, not merely with a love of compassion, which he did while they were yet in their sins, but with a love of ineffable complacency and delight. But (3) further, the Son seeing the Father rest with loving complacency on his disciple, feels himself drawn to that disciple by a new tie: 'And I will love him.' Mark here, I pray you, not only the sharp line of distinction between the divine persons, but also the *mutual* actings of each person respectively. The Father loves the disciple, because the disciple loves Jesus, and Jesus loves the disciple again, because the Father loves him. Whence arises (4) the clear revelation of himself, 'And will manifest myself unto him.' This is the highest fulfilment of the words: 'At that day ye shall know that I am in the Father, and ye in me, and I in you.' It is also the close of our Lord's reply to Philip's request, 'Show us the Father, and it sufficeth us' (verse 8).

But while this remarkable expression, 'And will manifest myself unto him,' winds up our Lord's answer to Philip's request, it also gives rise to another by Judas, which now follows: 'Judas saith unto him—not Iscariot —Lord, how is it'—what has happened—'that thou wilt manifest thyself unto us and not unto the world?' The Jude, or Judas, here mentioned is only elsewhere so called by Luke (6:16; Acts 1:13). In the lists of Matthew (10:3) and Mark (3:18) he is designated by the names of Lebbæus and Thaddæus. Observe here the peculiar care with which the Spirit of the Lord distinguishes this honoured servant from the traitor. He call him Judas, *not Iscariot*. The explanation, *not Iscariot*, may also be added to obviate the supposition of a return of Judas Iscariot, after he had once gone out (13:30). But however this may be, it is clear that this revelation, which Jesus had promised to his disciples—this distinction, which he had put between the church and the world— had perplexed the mind of this disciple. For he asks, as if in a tone of great surprise, what was the reason why Christ should manifest himself unto them, and not unto the world? 'Lord, what has happened? How comes it to pass, that thou wilt manifest thyself unto us, and not unto others?' And I have no doubt that it will be matter of eternal surprise to the redeemed in glory, why the Lord should have singled out them rather than others.

In our Lord's reply it is remarkable, that he continues his discourse very much as before: 'Jesus answered and said unto him, If a man love me, he will keep my words; and my Father will love him, and we will come unto him, and make our abode with him' (verse 23). It is evident that the first part of this verse is just a reproduction in another form of verse 21. And yet Jesus answers the question by repeating the promise as well as the conditions to which it is attached. Indeed, in one sense, there is a difference. The conditions of the promise are slightly abbreviated, while the promise itself is gloriously developed and enlarged; for instead of saying: 'I will love him, and manifest myself unto him,' it is now, 'We will come unto him, and make our abode with him.' And surely it is deeply significant to observe here that our Lord speaks of himself and the Father in such words as these—'*we* will come unto him.' Is not this '*we*' most wonderful? Does not the use of this term manifestly imply conscious equality with the Father? And may we not here say that wherever the Spirit of Christ is, *there are both the Father and the Son*? (Rom. 8:15). But what majestic words again are these—'And make our abode with him'! Is not this also most wonderful? The Father and the Son coming and taking up permanent, eternal abode with the soul! And moreover does not the term *'abode'* connect this verse with verse 2: 'In my Father's house are many mansions,' or *abodes*. Here on earth it is God who dwells with the believer; but yonder in the glory-land, it is the believer who is to dwell with God. The first of these facts is just the condition of the second. None shall dwell with God in heaven, with whom God does not first dwell on earth.

But our Lord answers not only the part of Jude's question which relates to the disciples, but also that which relates to the world: 'He that loveth me not keepeth not my sayings.' 'And it is no slight thing,' as if he said, 'to slight my word.' For, 'my word,' adds the Saviour, 'is not mine, hut his that sent me.' 'How then with such a disposition, hostile as it is to both the word of the Father and the Son, is it possible to make our abode with him?'

Such, then, is Christ's coming in the Spirit and its glorious results. And if there is one lesson more than another, which this passage is fitted to teach us, it is *the importance of the Spirit's work*. It was by the Spirit that he was to come to them, so as not to leave them 'orphans;' it was by the Spirit that they were to behold him through faith after his departure; it was by the Spirit they were to know the relation in which Jesus stood to the Father and to themselves; it was by the Spirit that he was to manifest himself unto them; and it was by the Spirit that the Father and the Son were to take up their eternal abode with them. Does not all this show us the unspeakable importance of the Spirit's work?

See also here *the great difference between the church and the world*. The blind world sees not now the glorified Christ; he is entirely beyond its reach. But to the spiritually enlightened disciple he is still visible by faith (verse 19). Let us earnestly ask ourselves, as in the presence of God, whether God has opened the eyes of our understanding to behold the Saviour's glory.

Further, let us learn here *the absolute safety of the church of God*. 'Because I live, ye shall live also.' Their fortunes stand or fall together. While the head lives in glory, there is no danger that the body shall perish. But there must be a connecting link between the head and the members. It will not do to say merely, Christ died but now lives, and therefore I shall live also. There must be a *vital union* between our souls and him by faith, or we must assuredly perish.

And, besides, do we not see here *the necessity of active practical love to Christ*? Who is he that the Father and the Son are to look upon with delight? To whom is the Son to manifest himself? And who is he, to whom the Father and the Son are to come and to take up their abode with for ever? It is he that loves Jesus and keeps his words. Oh! how close therefore the connection between holiness and the smile of God's face.

Lastly, let us be warned of *the danger of rejecting Christ's word*; for he that does, thus despises the authority of him that sent him (verse 24). And what is Christ's first word to each one of us? It is, 'Come unto me, all ye that labour and are heavy laden, and I will give you rest.' 'Look unto me, all ye ends of the earth, and be ye saved, for I am God.' Let us beware of despising him who thus speaks to us from heaven.

Special Consolations and Encouragements Suited to the Occasion

John 14:25–31

THE various instructions and consolations given by our Lord in the preceding context are very closely connected together, like so many links in a golden chain. First of all, he assures them that, although there was to be a separation for a time, yet there was afterwards to be a glorious reunion; and that, although he was now to leave them, yet it was only to prepare a place for them, and soon he would come again and fetch them home to himself (13:36; 14:3). Then, secondly, he was himself 'the way, the truth, and the life' (verse 6). He not only opened up the way, but as mediator between God and sinners, he was *himself* the way; so that if ever we reach heaven, we must come to it through himself; there must be a vital connection between him and us. And he is the way, not to heaven only, but in the first instance to the Father; for men do not come to heaven first, and then to the Father; but they come to the Father first, and then to heaven. Yea, he was at the same time the *revealer* of the Father. In him they had seen the Father already (verses 7–9), inasmuch as he was a partaker of the same nature and essence, as evinced by his words and works (verse 10). But this reference to his works brings out another idea. He now solemnly declares that he that believes on him shall do yet greater works than these—greater in the sense of being more spiritual in their nature—in their being instrumental in the conversion of souls—and this because he was going to the Father (verses 12, 13). For there, at the right hand of God, the enthroned Redeemer would answer all their prayers offered up in his name (verses 13, 14). There, too, he would pray the Father who would send them another Paraclete, who would enable them to pray, and by whose blessed agency those works of a higher character would be accomplished (verses 16, 17). But this reference to the Spirit—the other Paraclete—leads to another truth; he was not to leave them in the meantime 'orphans'; but he was soon to visit them in the presence and power of his Spirit, even here on earth; and this to prepare and qualify them for their eternal meeting in heaven.

Such, then, is the golden chain of heavenly truth presented to us in the preceding context.

And now our Lord brings to a close this first part of his discourse, by bringing before them some further consolations and encouragements suited to the occasion.

'These things'—the things already mentioned in the verses that go before—'have I spoken unto you, being yet present with you.' But then, referring to the time when he would not be present—to the time after his departure—he adds: 'But the Comforter'—the Paraclete—'which is the Holy Spirit, whom the Father will send in my name, he shall teach you all things, and bring all things to your remembrance, whatsoever I have said unto you.' The connection appears to be: 'This is what I can tell you now, but the Paraclete whom the Father will send in my name, *he* shall teach you all things,' etc.

As to the epithet 'holy,' which is here given to the Spirit, it seems to refer to the deep line of demarcation which he has drawn between the profane world and the disciples (verses 17–19); for as the Spirit of holiness he will dwell with those whom he has made fitting temples for himself. But what is the meaning of the words: 'Whom the Father will send *in my name*'? I think the full import embraces the three following things: On the ground of his finished work; in answer to his intercessory prayer; and also with his authority and power; for as the Son came in the Father's name, even so the Father was to send the Spirit in Jesus' name, that is, with like divine authority and power. And this word 'he' only brings out into stronger relief the instructions of the new teacher, as contrasted with those of Jesus, who was now to leave them. This divine Paraclete was to do two things. In the first place, he was to teach them 'all things'—not all things *absolutely*—but all things relating to the subject in hand—all things relating to faith and practice—all things belonging to your work and life in me—some of which cannot now be revealed. But he was also, secondly, to bring all things to their remembrance whatsoever Jesus had said unto them— thus reproducing in their souls what Jesus had already taught them—bringing up into living consciousness what lay like slumbering germs in their minds. Yea, the connection between those two things may be very close: 'He will teach you all things by bringing all things to your remembrance, whatsoever I have said unto you'— the sayings of Jesus, the memory of which the Holy Spirit would revive within them, being the subject-matter of all his instructions—the living germ which he would fertilise in their hearts.

But whatever may be said as to the connection between these two parts of this work, let us remember that on the fulfilment of this promise to the apostles, *the credibility and ultimate divine authority of the New Testament is founded.* We are sometimes flippantly and sneeringly asked by infidels and sceptics, how the apostles were able to remember all that Jesus said and did. 'Were they taking down notes at the time with pencil and tablets in hand?' No, indeed; nor did they need to. Most unquestionably the words and the works of Jesus were of such a character as to make a deep, yea, an indelible impression upon their hearts and memories. But over and above all this, they had the promise of the Holy Spirit to bring all things to their remembrance whatsoever Jesus had said. The memory of man at the best is but weak and treacherous; but the knowledge of the divine Spirit is unerring and infallible. Our faith rests not on the testimony of man, but on the power of God.

And yet something of the teaching of this Comforter, by bringing to remembrance, is experienced by every Christian who loves the Saviour and keeps his word. Not all at once does our understanding grasp the whole word of God, but if we truly love it and honour it, then, in his own good time, the Spirit will come, and reveal to our hearts, and bring to our memories just those particular truths and sayings which are the most salutary and comforting in our particular case. And what hours of joy are those which we then experience!

But our Lord now pronounces upon them his parting words of *blessing*: 'Peace I leave with you, my peace I give unto you,' etc. (verse 27). It was the custom in Israel, both in meeting and in parting, to greet one another by wishing peace (1 Sam. 1:17). And just so the Lord of glory, before his departure, will say, 'Peace I leave with you'—peace I bequeath unto you as a dying legacy. But oh, how infinitely different from ordinary adieus! For who can tell how much is wrapped up in that peace? 'My peace,' says Jesus. As the Prince of Peace, he brought it with him into this world (Isa. 9:6), carried it about with him in his own blessed person, died to purchase it for us, left it as a dying legacy to his disciples upon earth, and now lives to apply it to their souls. Well, therefore, may it be called 'my peace.' It is a legacy derived from his own treasury; it is his own peace that Christ gives us. But that expression: 'I give'—how significant! Ah! many a legacy is left that never reaches the legatee, many a gift is designed that is never bestowed on its proper object. But Christ is not only the testator, but the executor of his own will and testament. The peace that he bequeaths, he also bestows. And thus all is safe—all is placed beyond the possibility of his people coming short of it.

And then, that other word: 'Not as the world giveth give I unto you'—Oh how precious! The contrast is between the world's manner of giving and Christ's. The world gives *grudgingly*, *deceitfully*; Christ gives *cheerfully*, *sincerely*. The world gives you but *empty words*, a *mere powerless wish*, when it says, 'Peace be unto you'; but Christ's gift is *real*, *substantial*, and *efficacious*. The world's good wishes can, at the best, extend *only to the life that now is*; Christ's blessing is *eternal*.

No wonder, therefore, though he repeats the exhortation: 'Let not your heart be troubled, neither let it be afraid.' These were, substantially, the words of consolation with which he opened up this part of the discourse, and now he addresses them in the same words at the close of it. Yea, he assigns the same reason for it as before: 'Ye have heard how I said unto you, I go away and come again to you' (verse 28). Indeed, this may be said to be the keynote of this whole chapter: 'I go, but I come again.'

But it was not enough for Jesus that they should not be troubled nor afraid; he would also have them positively to *rejoice*: 'If ye love me, ye would rejoice, because I said, I go unto the Father; for my Father is greater than I.' The words: 'If ye loved me,' are exquisitely tender. The Saviour appeals to their love to him; he would have them to rejoice in his going to the Father, from *the very love* which they felt to him. And for this reason: that the Father, to whom he was going, was greater than he. And without entering here on the controversy which has raged around these words, it is quite sufficient for my purpose to remark that Christ is not speaking here of the filial relation in which he stood to the Father, but of his relation as the God-Man-Mediator. In this respect, the Father was greater than the Son; and therefore the going to the Father was an advancement; and if they loved him, they ought to rejoice in this. What true friend would not rejoice to see his friend exalted to a position of dignity and honour? And in like manner, if they loved Jesus, they ought to rejoice in his going to the Father; for it was his advancement as Mediator to a position of the highest dignity and glory. The same thing may be said, in a subordinate sense, of Christian friends, who have slept in Jesus. However painful the separation may be to us, yet if we truly loved them, we would rejoice because they have gone to be with Christ.

But now our blessed Lord gives the reason why he told them of these things beforehand. Oh, it was not because he desired to give them pain, but for their spiritual benefit: 'And now, I have told you before it come to pass, that when it is come to pass, ye might believe,' that is, in the fullest sense, 'that I am he' (verse 29). This painful separation and this return of his, which they now find it so difficult to receive, when they would actually take place, and the disciples would remember the present sayings of Jesus, would greatly tend to their establishment in the faith.

But now approaching still more closely to the painful subject of his departure, he adds: 'Hereafter I will not talk much with you' (verse 30). He had, indeed, some more words to say; he was not to break off altogether at verse 31. But he was not to talk much to them after this. And why? 'For the prince of this world cometh'— not Judas merely, but Satan himself, with whom the Lord of glory was in conflict during his passion (Luke 22:53). He had obviously a presentiment not only of the coming of Judas, but also of the conflict with Satan himself, which he was to sustain in Gethsemane. But what a testimony: 'And hath nothing in me'—nothing of his own—nothing on which to fasten his arrows (Heb. 9:14; 1 John 3:5; 2 Cor. 5:21). 'But,' adds the Saviour, 'that the world may know that I love the Father,' etc. (verse 31). And, notwithstanding all that has been said about these words, as being elliptical and so forth, I am disposed to take them up in their simple and natural meaning, connecting the words, 'that the world may know' with the last words of the sentence: 'Arise, let us go hence.' It is just as if he had said, 'The prince of this world hath nothing in me—no sin on which to fasten his attack—but, that the world may know that my death is voluntary, that I love the Father, and that as the Father gave me commandment, even so I do, arise, let us go hence' (Matt 9:6). Thus to arise, for the purpose of going to Gethsemane, was in fact voluntarily to surrender himself to the power of Satan, who was then preparing for the decisive conflict; and to the treachery of Judas, who was about to seek him in the well-known place. And so at last he gives the summons to depart, for which he had already prepared them.

But this at once raises the question, Did they, or did they not, at this stage of the discourse, arise and leave the supper room?—a somewhat delicate question, which has been keenly canvassed on both sides. On the one hand, it has been supposed by many able interpreters, that they remained in the upper room till after the intercessory prayer; that if the summons to arise was literally responded to by the guests, a mere wave of the hand would be enough to show that there was more to follow, ere they broke up; and that probably the rest of the discourse and the prayer (chapter 17) were spoken when all were now standing ready to depart. While, on the other hand, it has been as keenly contended by others that at this point of the discourse they arose and left the supper room. The question is not certainly one of any very great intrinsic importance; but, as your attention is sure to be directed to it, it may not be out of place that I should indicate briefly, why I am inclined to adopt the latter view. And surely, in the first instance, when our Lord said: 'Arise, let us go hence,' it is the most natural thing to suppose that they did so, especially when there is nothing said to the contrary. Or, if we suppose that they still remained, then, in that case, it is difficult to perceive why the apostle should have so expressly mentioned this order for removal, without giving the slightest hint or explanation of the delay. I should be disposed, on this account alone, to believe that they did now move. But what tends to confirm this idea, secondly, is that we are elsewhere told (Matt. 26:30) that they went to the Mount of Olives before they entered into the garden of Gethsemane. Then, if so, with the vineyards of Olivet before them, we seem to have got a natural explanation of the figure of the vine and the branches. Further, this view seems to account, partly at least, for the difference in form between the two different parts of the discourse. And lastly, it is said in 17:1 that 'Jesus lifted up his eyes to heaven.' How much more natural this action if understood of something done out of doors, than on the idea that they were still in the upper room. On these grounds, I am disposed to think that Jesus having given the signal for departure (verse 31), we must regard the discourse of chapters 15 and 16, as well as the intercessory prayer in chapter 17, as having been delivered somewhere on the slopes of Mount Olivet, leading to the valley of the Kedron.

But, without occupying more of your time with this question, it is of the utmost importance for us to learn from the passage, which has just been examined, *the divine authority of the New Testament Scriptures*. For surely it is plainly taught in the words of Jesus: 'But the Comforter shall teach you all things, and bring all things to your remembrance, whatsoever I have said unto you.' And when once the inspiration and divine authority of the New Testament is settled, that of the Old Testament necessarily follows; for the books of the Old Testament are quoted and referred to in the New, in such a way as to show that they are stamped with divine approval, and are of divine authority.

Secondly, let us observe here *the unspeakable blessedness of the church of God*. For who can tell what is wrapped up in the peace which Jesus bestows? The Lord save each one of us from a false peace! but of the peace which Jesus gives, you never can partake too largely.

Further, let the children of Zion be joyful in their King; let them rejoice that he has gone to the Father—that he is now glorified. I do not know whether many of us drink deeply out of this well of consolation, if indeed we drink out of it at all; but I will venture to say that there is not a sweeter joy on this side of heaven, than when the Christian is enabled to rejoice that his Redeemer is glorified, that he now sees, and will continue to see, of the travail of his soul until he is perfectly satisfied.

Finally, what an insight have we here into *the Saviour's character*. The prince of this world indeed had nothing in him—nothing on which he could work. No, but we see in Jesus love to the Father, and obedience to his commandment, even when that commandment involved his laying down his life for the sheep. 'Arise, let us go hence.' 'I have a baptism to be baptised with, and how am I straitened until it be accomplished.' The Lord give us to have this love shed abroad in our hearts by the Holy Ghost given to us!

[B]

The State, Duties and Prospects of the Disciples in the World

John 15:1–16:15

The Vine and the Branches
John 15:1–8

THE part of our Lord's discourse to which we have now come differs considerably in *form* from that which has already been examined. The latter—that which we have gone over—partakes largely of the character of a loving, familiar conversation, in which Jesus replies to certain questions put to him by some of his disciples. But from this point onwards his instructions assume more the form of one continuous, sustained discourse until you reach chapter 16:17; when the dialogue-form again appears. But more than this—not only is there a difference in form between these two parts, but there is also a very remarkable difference as to *matter* or *substance*. The great leading theme of the preceding conversations is that although there was to be a parting for a time, yet there was afterwards to be a meeting, ultimately indeed, in heaven, but previously also upon the earth, by the indwelling of his Spirit. But here—in the part that now lies before us—he takes up rather the condition of his disciples in the world after his departure, their duties and responsibilities, their difficulties and dangers, and withal their glorious encouragements. Hence three leading ideas come up here prominently before us: (1) Their relations to Christ and to one another (verses 1–17), (2) Their relations to the world (verse 18–16:4); and (3) Their relation to the Holy Spirit (16:5–15). These are the three great subjects that come up here successively to view—their relations to Christ and to one another, their relations to the world—the sinful world that lies in the wicked one— and the promise of the Holy Spirit expanded in all its fullness. But for the present we confine ourselves to the relation between *Christ and his people*, as beautifully illustrated by the figure of the vine and the branches.

When our Lord said to his disciples: 'Arise, let us go hence,' they immediately left the supper room, as we believe, passed in silence through the streets of Jerusalem, and soon found themselves in some secluded spot on the slopes of Mount Olivet leading to the valley of the Kedron. And there, surrounded by his little band of disciples, he sees a beautiful emblem of himself, 'I am the true vine, and my Father is the husbandman.' Here, then, we have, first, *the groundwork of the parable* (verses 1–3), then, secondly, *the duty and necessity of abiding in the vine* (verse 4), and, thirdly, *the consequences of the fulfilment or the neglect of this duty* (verses 4–8).

[1] With reference to the first of these, Jesus says, 'I am the true vine'—I myself—not means and ordinances

merely, but I myself in my person and work. When Jesus said, 'I am the true vine,' we are naturally led to suppose that he here intends to contrast himself with some other vine, which was not in his eyes the true one, but only an image of it. And when we ask what that external vine was, which led Jesus thus to express himself, those who maintain that they had not yet quitted the supper room, either decline to answer the question altogether, or else have recourse to various suppositions, which are altogether forced and fanciful. But if it be admitted, as we think it ought to be, that Jesus and his disciples had ere this time left the supper room, then the explanation becomes simple, and easy, and beautiful. 'I,' says the divine Redeemer, with the vines of Olivet before him—'I am the true, the essential, spiritual vine, of which that earthly one is but an image.'

And if I were now asked, wherein lies the precise point of resemblance between Christ and the vine, I would say, it is in that *mysterious oneness*, in consequence of which the life of the vine-stock becomes that of the branches. For just as it is the same life and sap that abides in the vine and in the branches, so it is the same life which in its surpassing glory and fullness dwells in the God-Man-Mediator that is also in the weakest believer. It is the same Spirit, poured out upon the head, and received by him without measure, that in measure is given to his people. And this is peculiar to the work of our salvation, as peculiar to it as is incarnation or substitution. I suppose that holiness, as to the substance of it, is the same in the holy angels as it is in Christians; yea, that it is the same in *the nature* of it in his people, as it is in God himself. But herein lies the peculiarity of the life of God's people that the God-Man is the spring of it; that it is his life-giving power that creates it at the first, that preserves it, and that causes it to grow from grace to grace, and from grace to glory. Hence arises a *peculiarly close dependence* of Christ's people upon Christ. And hence also their blessed security in having their life bound up with his: 'Because I live,' says he, 'ye shall live also.'

And while Jesus is thus 'the true vine'—the source of his people's spiritual life and fruitfulness—his Father is 'the husbandman', that is, the great proprietor of the vineyard, and its cultivator. The title of husbandman is given to God as at once the owner and the vinedresser. He it is who possesses it, and who watches over it with peculiar care. Jesus doubtless intends to impress upon them the value of this plant, which God himself tends and watches over with such care.

And the *manner* in which he *cultivates* the vine is thus referred to: 'Every branch in me that beareth not fruit he taketh away,' etc. (verse 2). It is plainly implied in these words that there are *two* sets of branches in the vine—fruitful and fruitless ones. For just as in a fruit tree some branches may be fruitful, while others are quite barren, according as there is a *vital connection*, or *no vital connection* between the branches and the vine-stock; so the professing followers of Christ may be spiritually fruitful, or the reverse, according as they are spiritually and vitally united to Christ, or but externally and mechanically attached to him. In drawing this two-fold sketch, our Lord has evidently in view not only his disciples, but his future church; and he gives us plainly to understand that as in it there would be always some fruit-bearing Christians, because of his dwelling in them by his Spirit, so there would also be fruitless ones, because, while externally united to him, they would nevertheless be internally separated from him. Oh, with what earnestness, therefore, should each one of us enquire whether we are spiritually united to Christ, or simply artificially tied to him by a bare profession of his name or an outward adherence to his cause!

For see, in the second instance here, *how the divine husbandman deals with these branches respectively.* The one—that which does not bear fruit—*he takes away*, sometimes in the present life, either by prosperity or by adversity (Matt. 13:21, 22.) But whether in this life or not—whether he will do it by prosperity or by adversity here, or not—there is a time coming that shall bring to the test every Christless professor. Yes, solemn truth! every fruitless branch the divine husbandman shall remove from its place in the vineyard—in the hour of death and of judgment. For thus it is written: 'Every plant which my heavenly Father hath not planted shall be rooted up' (Matt. 15:13).

But, on the other hand, the fruitful branch '*he pur-geth*'—cleanseth, or pruneth—stripping it, as the husbandman does, of what is rank and luxuriant, free-ing it from those barren shoots and useless tendrils that absorb the sap, and hinder real fruitfulness—a process often painful, but not the less needful and beneficial than in the natural husbandry. And various are the ways in which he does it—by the word of his grace (verse 3), by the dealings of his providence, by afflictions and chastisements, and, above all, by the effectual opera-tion of his Spirit: 'If ye through the Spirit do mortify the deeds of the body, ye shall live.' But whatever be the means, the *design* is the same, 'that it may bring forth more fruit.' It is not to weaken or impair the principle of fruitfulness that he prunes, far less to destroy it; but it is to render it more fruitful. And yet we do not always see the reason of this; we sometimes marvel when we see the child of God subjected to the pruning-knife of the heavenly husbandman. But here is the true explana-tion of it: his heavenly Father would have that child to become more and more fruitful; and therefore he takes his pruning-knife in hand, and strikes off what is hin-dering real growth. Ah! this is the reason why the most eminent saints have often been the most deeply tried; the great measure of their fruitfulness they acquired in the school of sanctified affliction.

And just as if to calm the minds of his disciples with respect to this operation, Jesus reminds them (verse 3) that in their case it is already accomplished: 'Now ye are clean through the word which I have spoken unto you.' The emphasis is to be laid on the word 'now'—already.

And how did they attain to this? It was in consequence of the long action upon them of that word, which is 'as a refiner's fire' (Mal. 3:2).

[2] But from this general view of the case, our Lord now proceeds to speak of *the duty and necessity of abiding in the vine*, as the great secret of fruit-bearing: 'Abide in me, and I in you' (verse 4).

And certainly the duty, which is here enjoined, pre-supposes as lying at the very root of it *a vital spiritual union to Christ*. It is impossible to *abide* in him, unless we are first of all *in* him—vitally united to him by faith. When our Lord exhorts believers to abide in him, this is not to be understood as implying that any soul that is truly in Christ ever afterwards falls away from him finally and irrecoverably. No indeed, the teaching of Scripture is the very reverse of this. But then, on the other hand, how am I to know that I was ever truly in him, except by abiding in him? Is it not manifestly our duty to abide in him? And do we not need all the warnings and exhortations that can be addressed on this head? Yes, our *first* care must be to get an interest in Christ, and our *continued* care must be to abide in him. Is there some soul here who, from his own blessed experience, can remember a time when he was long seeking rest, and finding none, but who at last found it in Jesus? Oh, how deep the sense of personal unworthiness then! How vivid the impression of the Saviour's glory and preciousness then! Well, to such a soul Jesus says: 'Abide in me.'

But still the question is, what is it to abide in Christ? It implies, for one thing, *a continued sense of need of him*. The poverty of spirit to which the blessing is attached by our Lord, is characteristic of the Christian, not at the outset of his course only, but while he is in this world. Oh! brethren, beware of that religion that dispenses with the necessity of poverty of spirit. But it implies also *an abiding perception of Christ's all-sufficiency and glory*. Without this the Christian, with his deep exercise, would be of all men the most miserable. But if the blessedness of the poor in spirit lies in this, that theirs is the kingdom of heaven to enrich them, the blessedness of the Christian growing in poverty of spirit lies in this, that *Christ is his*, to be more and more known by him in his unsearchable riches. Further, to abide in Christ is *to depend upon him—to trust in him* for all that is needed to maintain and perfect the divine life—for wisdom, righteousness, and strength—for renewing and sanctifying grace. To abide in Christ is *to adhere to him*—to his blessed person, to his truth, to his cause, and to his people; and this, too, notwithstanding all temptations to depart from him. In a word, to abide in Christ, is to abide in him *to the end*—till the soul can go no more out, till it be made white in his blood, and be filled with all the fullness of God.

And this union, you observe, is *mutual*. For just as truly as the soul is to abide in Christ, so Christ is to abide in the soul. 'Abide in me, and *I in you*.' Oh, what a mysterious union is this! Christ in the soul through the indwelling Spirit, and the soul in Christ by faith. Christ in heaven and the soul on earth, and yet both so united that they are said to be the one in the other.

[3] But now, thirdly, and just as if to enforce this duty, our Lord sets before them *the consequences of the fulfilment, or the neglect of this duty* (verses 4–8).

And here he mentions first *the impossibility of bearing fruit*, except by abiding in the vine: 'As the branch cannot bear fruit of itself except it abide in the vine, no more can ye except ye abide in me' (verse 4). For a branch to abide in the vine is the condition, the very law of its life. All the conditions of fruitfulness are included in this. And just so it is impossible—absolutely impossible—for the believer to bear fruit, except as he abides in Christ Jesus.

And indeed the words which follow: 'I am the true vine, ye are the branches' (verse 5), are not, as has been said by some, a vain, useless repetition, or a mere tardy development of the truth expressed in verse 1. But, on the contrary, by this repetition he would impress on his disciples a deeper sense of their absolute dependence upon him; he would emphasise it in their hearing. 'Ah, yes, this is indeed what I am to you: "I am the vine, ye are the branches."'

But then, just as if to set *the momentous consequences involved* still more clearly before us, he draws a *vivid contrast* between the case of the man that abides in him and that of the man who does not (verses 5, 6). With reference to the one he says: 'He that abideth in me and

I in him, the same bringeth forth much fruit'—not only fruit, but *much* fruit. And oh, what lovely fruit does such a branch bear! The very fruit that grows on the vine! The soul that abides in Christ by faith *resembles* Christ in all the lovely graces of his character. And the reason assigned for this: 'For without me'—separate from me—'ye can do nothing,' that is, nothing spiritually good—oh, what a strange reason is this! If these words were adduced as a statement or explanation of the fact that apart from him they could bear *no* fruit, we should at once see the force of them; but assigned as a reason for their bearing *much* fruit, they seem strange words indeed. But then, if Christ be *all* to his people in such a glorious and comprehensive sense that *without* him they can do *nothing*, does it not plainly follow, on the other hand, that '*through Christ strengthening them, they can do all things*'? This is what Jesus says of him that abides in him, and this is the reason which he gives for his bearing much fruit.

But then, in terrible contrast with this case, he puts that of the man who does *not* abide in him (verse 6): 'If a man abide not in me, he is cast forth, and is withered,' etc. Here are five successive steps in the judgment: (1) 'he is cast forth'—out of the vineyard, over the garden wall; (2) 'and is withered'; the cast-out branch withers; (3) 'and men gather them'—the vineyard labourers—in the application the angels (Matt. 13:41); (4) 'and cast them into the fire'—the terrible emblem of judgment; (5) 'and they are burned,' or rather, they burn; it is the present tense which has its full force, denoting constant duration. These are the five steps in the judgment, the complete execution of which is, by God's longsuffering, delayed. The first two steps—the being cast forth and the withering—lie within the limits of this mortal life; the third step—the gathering of the withered branches— lies on the borderline between time and eternity; and the two last steps—'cast into the fire and they burn'— are laid in eternity. The only use for which the withered branches are fitted is to burn. Oh! how awfully solemn, in this view of it, is this parable!

But our Lord will not close with this terrible description. He returns to the case of the man that abides in Christ: 'If ye abide in me and my words abide in you,' etc. (verse 7). Mark here the change from *his* dwelling in them to that of *his words*. The parallelism would lead us to expect the words to run thus, as in verse 4: 'If ye abide in me and I in you.' But instead of this, he now says: 'And my words abide in you.' In fact, it is by continually remembering and meditating on the words of Jesus that the disciples continue united to Jesus, and that he continues to act on earth by his disciples. But with this Jesus now connects another idea, namely that of *prayers*: 'Ye shall ask what ye will.' Indeed the words of Jesus, digested by meditation, nourish in the soul of the believer those holy desires which urge to prayer. Such a prayer is a product of divine grace; it is God's promise turned into a petition, and it is sure to be heard, because this indwelling of his word secures the harmony of our askings with the will of God. 'If ye abide in me, and *my words* abide in you, ye shall ask what ye will and it shall be done unto you.'

And the issue of the whole matter is that 'herein is the Father glorified, that ye bear much fruit' (verse 8). What could be more honouring to the husbandman than the abundant fruitfulness of the vine that he had watched over with such tender care? 'So shall ye be my disciples'; that is, evidence—prove yourselves—to be my disciples.

Such, then, is the parable of the vine and the branches. And now, on a review of the whole, let us learn from it, first, *what Christ is to his people*—the source of their life and fruitfulness; their life is bound up with his. But in order to this, there must be *a vital connection* between him and us; we must become living branches in the living vine. See also here an *emblem of the visible church*. It consists of fruitless as well as fruitful branches—of nominal as well as real Christians. And yet the fact that there are fruitless branches in the vine does *not* destroy the connection between Christ and his true people. Let us see here also *the necessity of self-examination*. For oh, how infinite the difference between these two kinds of branches! How great the difference here, and how great must it be in the other world! Let us see to it that there be no mistake here.

How important that we should manifest *the reality of our faith by our abiding in him*. If there is one lesson more than another, which is here most earnestly impressed on us, it is the duty and necessity of *abiding* in Christ. Not less than seven different times does our Lord mention it within the compass of a few verses. And so deeply was it engraven on the heart of the Apostle John that, in his first Epistle, all his exhortations to Christians converge on this as their centre—abiding in him (1 John 2:3–6). Let us see to it, therefore, that we abide in him. It is only thus that we can bring forth fruit, even the fruit by which the Father is glorified. Alas! we are so prone to seek our fruitfulness anywhere else than in Christ; but as well might you expect the earth to clothe itself with verdure without the warm sunshine and the genial showers of heaven, as that a soul can bear fruit except as it abides in the vine. Here is the very fatness of our souls—abiding in Christ. 'Abide in me and I in you.'

Lastly, *how sad the case of one who once seemed to be in Christ*—a believer in his name, and an ardent lover of his people, his cause, and his truth—but who has since shown that he was never *truly* in him! Oh! if there be one such here, may the Lord in his infinite mercy awaken him, ere it be too late! And it is the unspeakable privilege of such to know that he invites you to come to him, with the blessed assurance that, coming to him, he will in no wise cast you out. Apprehend the grace of so blessed an invitation, and do not tarry from coming; and so you shall enter into peace.

Abiding in the Love of Christ by Keeping His Commandments

John 15:9–17

IN the first verse of this most precious and most beautiful passage, we have *a comparison drawn between the Father's love to the Son, and the Son's love to the disciples*, and then *a duty, an exhortation*, founded upon it. And the one will go far in enabling us to understand the other.

In the first instance, as to *the comparison*, Jesus says: 'As the Father hath loved me,' etc., or rather: 'Even as the Father hath loved me, I also have loved you.' The pith of this wonderful statement lies in the words 'Even as'—'so.' What, then, is the love wherewith the Father loves the Son? Not surely the love of pity and compassion, but that of *complacency and delight*. Of the like nature is the love of Jesus to his people. It is true indeed, that he loved them with a love of pity and compassion, when they were in their low and lost estate—when they were in the filthiness of sin; but it is also a most blessed truth that ever since he made them 'his own' by his effectual grace—ever since he clothed them with his righteousness and made them the temples of his Holy Spirit—he regards them with peculiar satisfaction and delight. For it is the Lord's way, first, in his infinite mercy, to make his people comely through his comeliness put upon them, and then to take delight in them.

Now it is this love of complacency and delight on the part of Jesus in which we are here exhorted to 'continue,' or rather to 'abide.' It is not 'abide in the exercise of love *to* me'—although that is a most important duty in itself—but it is 'abide under the influence of my love to you'. In fact, the expression 'my love' can only mean here the love of Jesus to his people. Jesus now substitutes the idea of abiding in his love for that of abiding in himself. And it is just as if he had said: 'Abide under the sweet smiles of my love to you.'

And that this is the meaning of the exhortation is equally clear from the words which follow. For our Lord proceeds to show them the condition of abiding in his love: 'If ye keep my commandments, ye shall abide in my love' (verse 10). What, then, is the love of Jesus, which we secure to ourselves, by the keeping of his commandments? Not surely the love of pity and compassion; for in that respect he loved us before we were capable of keeping his commandments; yea, while we were yet in our sins. But, on the other hand, the keeping of his commandments in the spirit of true filial obedience does bring down upon the soul the sunshine of the Saviour's smile.

And our Lord points out to them that he imposes upon them no other condition with respect to himself, than that to which *he himself cheerfully submitted with reference to the Father*: 'Even as I have kept my Father's commandments and abide in his love.' His whole life was one continuous course of obedience to the divine will, and this was the glorious secret of his abiding in his Father's love. Such also is the position of the believer with respect to Christ's love to him. The condition of his abiding in the love of Christ—under the sunshine of his smile and approbation—is the keeping of his commandments.

And moreover, the *end* that Jesus had in view in saying these things unto them, is thus clearly pointed out: 'These things have I spoken unto you that my joy might remain in you, and that your joy might be full' (verse 11). 'My joy,' says the divine Redeemer: what is the joy of which he here speaks? It is not merely the joy that he *would produce in them*—the joy of which he is the *author*; neither is it the joy which he feels *on their account*; but it is the joy which *he experiences* in knowing himself to be the object of his Father's love. That this is the idea is obvious enough (1) from the connection. He has just been speaking of abiding in the Father's love, by keeping his commandments, and then he proceeds to speak of his joy. Does not this imply that the joy of which he speaks is that which he experiences in abiding in the Father's love? And the same thing is equally clear (2) from the words themselves: 'That my joy might remain in you'; it was to be *in them*—to be *experienced by them*. Hence it plainly follows that the joy of Christ and the joy of his people—'your joy'—were not to be two different joys; but his joy was to become theirs. Oh! how beautiful! how precious! The joy of Christ—the very joy which he experienced in abiding in his Father's love—was to be, in their measure, reproduced in their hearts, in the way of obedience to his commandments. And this joy might grow by obedience to perfect fullness: 'That your joy might be full.'

But our blessed Lord now *concentrates* this obedience to which he exhorts and invites them, *in the one exercise of brotherly love*. 'This is my commandment, that ye love one another' (verse 12). It just reminds one of the first charge, which he gave them after enunciating his own departure: 'A new commandment I give unto you, that ye love one another.' And the reason, the model, that he sets before them is also the same: 'As I have loved you.'

But then, just as if to set forth the fullness and beauty of this model, Jesus supplies a commentary on his own words (verse 13–16). Three great truths are here presented to us: First, *the greatness* of his love, or the *extent* to which love carries its devotion, viz., *death* (verse 13); then, secondly, *the intimacy*, the familiar character of it; he has shown towards them the intimate relation of a friend, rather than the authority of an austere master (verses 14, 15); and thirdly, he shows them *the origin* of this relation; it was he that took the initiative in establishing it (verse 16). Let us briefly look at these three points in their order.

In the first instance, Jesus speaks here of *the greatness* of his love, or *the extent* to which it would carry him: 'Greater love hath no man than this, that a man lay down his life for his friends' (verse 13). Undoubtedly there is, *absolutely* speaking, a greater proof of love than this, viz., to give one's life for one's enemies, and Jesus did this. 'For scarcely for a righteous man will one die: yet peradventure for a good man some would even dare to die. But God commendeth his love towards us, in that, while we were yet sinners, Christ died for us.' But Christ is here speaking of the relation of friendship; and certainly in this respect there is no greater proof of love than the sacrifice of life. A man can show no greater regard for those dear to him than to give his life for them, and such love would they find in Jesus!

But, secondly, he adverts to *the close and familiar character of the relation to which he had admitted them.* 'Ye are my friends, if ye do whatsoever I command you' (verse 14). As if our Lord meant to say to them: 'It was not without good reason that I just now said, "for his friends," for this is really the relation in which I stand to you, if ye do whatsoever I command you.' And what is there more beautiful in domestic life than when a master, who finds a servant truly faithful, raises him to the rights and title of a friend? Such was what Jesus had done for them. And just as if to prove the reality of this statement, he adds: 'Henceforth I call you not servants.' There is, indeed, a sense in which he still calls them servants (verse 20), and in which they delight to call themselves so—the sense, I mean, of being under law to Christ (1 Cor. 9:21)—but he does not call them or treat them as servants in the way of withholding from them the secret of his love, as he proceeds immediately to explain: 'For the servant knoweth not what his lord doeth'—knows nothing of his plans and reasons, but simply receives and executes his orders; 'but I have called you friends, for all things that I have heard of the Father I have made known unto you.' He had admitted them into unbounded confidence, revealing to them what the Father had revealed to him, in so far as they were able to take them in. Undoubtedly there were many things of which they were not informed; but it was not from want of confidence in them and love to them that he had not revealed these also, but because they were not able to bear them now, and because another only could fulfil the task.

And then, lastly, he points out *the origin* of this relation; it was not they but he that took the initiative: 'Ye have not chosen me, but I have chosen you'—a most wholesome lesson—a most salutary and humbling lesson, after all the lofty things he had just said regarding the privileges to which they were admitted. If they had been peculiarly favoured, the glory of this was due not to them but to him. And while the expressions—'chosen' and 'appointed' you—may contain a reference, as in 6:70

and 13:18, to the solemn act of their appointment to the apostolic office, it is also true of their eternal salvation, that the initiative was of his own free and spontaneous grace. 'I have chosen you,' says he, 'and appointed you, that ye should go and bring forth fruit'—that is, give yourselves to it, and make it your business—'and that your fruit should abide'—showing itself to be an imperishable, ever-growing principle. And to this Jesus adds the means by which they were to accomplish this task—namely, prayer in his name: 'That whatsoever ye shall ask of the Father in my name, he shall give it you.'

Such, then, is the model which Jesus sets before us for our love. It is just as if he had said to them and to us: 'If you ask yourselves what limits you are to lay to your love to one another, first ask yourselves what limits I put to the love that I have shown to you.' Or, 'If you wish to know what it is to love, look at me and my love.'

And now, having set his own love before them as the great model, he repeats the commandment in a most emphatic form: 'These things I command you that ye love one another, (verse 17)—as if he had said to them: 'This is the sum and substance of all that I have now said to you, that ye love one another.'

Thus have I tried to bring out to you, in a brief and simple way, the scope of the Saviour's teaching in this passage. The successive steps in the chain of instruction might now be summarised thus: (1) First of all, as the

Father loves the Son with an ineffable love of delight, so the Son loves his own people that are in him; it is the duty and privilege of the children of God to abide under the influence of this love. (2) The *condition* of abiding under the influence of Christ's love is the keeping of his commandments. It was by keeping the Father's commandments that Jesus abode in his love; and it is by keeping Christ's commandments that we must abide in his love. (3) The *result* of keeping his commandments is true heavenly joy. This spirit of filial obedience is the pathway, the royal road to real joy and happiness: 'That my joy might abide in you.' That is to say—the very joy which Christ himself experienced would be produced and sustained in them. (4) The commandments, to the obedience of which he summons them, are all concentrated in the one great commandment of *brotherly love.* (5) But just as if to press home and recommend this duty, he sets before them his own example. His love to them was so great, so close, and withal so free and spontaneous. Let this be their *model* and their *motive* to love one another.

This I take to be the main scope of this passage. And when we take this whole section together, from the beginning of this chapter, the substance of it may be briefly stated thus: *Abiding in Christ as the source of all spiritual fruitfulness, and abiding in his love, by keeping his commandments.* That is to say, *faith in Christ himself* and *obedience to him*, especially in the duty of brotherly love—faith in Christ, in short, and love to the brethren. The Lord enable us so to believe, and believing, to love the brethren! For 'this is his commandment, that we should believe on the name of his Son Jesus Christ, and love one another, as he gave us commandment' (1 John 3:23).

The Disciples Hated by the World, Like Their Master, and for His Sake

John 15:18–25

IN the preceding section of this chapter, our Lord brings before us the relation in which his disciples were to stand to him and to one another. Their relation to him was to be one of *faith* and *obedience*—abiding in Christ, and abiding in his love by keeping his commandments, especially the great commandment that they should love one another: and therefore, their relation to one another, springing out of the former, was to be that of *mutual love*. But in dark and dismal contrast to this, he now proceeds to warn them of the hatred and hostility of the world—the world that lies in the wicked one, and which was at the time represented by the Jewish people. If the friends and disciples of the Lord Jesus were to be distinguished by their adherence to him and to one another, they were, at the same time, to be not the less marked out as the objects of the world's hatred. To this painful subject our Lord refers in the passage now under consideration. And then, after encouraging his disciples by a passing reference to the glorious Comforter, or Advocate, whom he was to send them from the Father (verses 26, 27), he returns to the same subject, and sets before them, in darker colours than before, what they had reason to expect from the world (16:1–4).

Let me, therefore, on the present occasion, endeavour to draw your attention to what is here said of the *world's hatred*. Our Lord refers to this painful subject, not merely to announce the fact, but to fortify their minds against the day of trial; and this he does in a twofold way—first, by reminding them that it hated him *before* it hated them; and then, by declaring, that the world's hatred of them would be *for his sake* (verses 21–25). Surely there could be nothing better fitted to prepare them for suffering—to incite them to endure hardness as good soldiers of Jesus Christ—than the thought that they were called to suffer like their Master and for his sake.

[1] With reference to the first of these ideas, when Jesus says: 'If the world hate you,' etc., we are not to understand these words as implying that there was any doubt or uncertainty as to their being hated by the world. On the contrary, we know that it will be so; yea, that it *must* be so, so long as the world remains the world, and Christians remain Christians; so long as the race of Cains and the race of Abels continue on

the earth. But then here is the truth to which he would direct their hearts: 'If the world hate you, ye know,' or rather, 'know,' in the imperative, 'that it hated me before it hated you.' Consider, as if he said, what took place in my case, and ye will be less surprised at what shall take place in your own. Ah! yes, the world hated Christ, and therefore, what can his followers expect but to be treated in just the same way.

And then our Lord next proceeds to explain the *ground* of the world's hatred, which would bring additional comfort, inasmuch as it would afford clear evidence that they were not of this world, but endued with a higher life: 'If ye were of the world'—if ye were of its spirit and principles—'the world would love his own'—that which belongs to it. That is the world's way. And therefore, if the world—the sinful, unrenewed world—loves you, it is because it sees in you its own, and claims you for its property. Oh, if we could only see to the bottom of this matter, we should perceive with horror that whatever there may be in us that is pleasing to the sinful world, belongs to the flesh. Be rebuked, therefore, and put to shame by the sinful world, it if loves you, and cast out of you whatever it finds to love. But, on the other hand, says our Lord: 'Because ye are not of the world,' etc. He states *a fact*, he declares that they were not of the world. And how did this come about? They were once of the world, children of wrath, even as others. And if so, how comes it to pass that they are not now of the world? Did they rescue themselves from its iron grasp? Oh, no, but their merciful God and Saviour *had chosen them out of it*—and this not by his electing love only, but by his effectual grace, drawing them into his family—not to be apostles merely, but to be believers, members of his body. Let us constantly remember this truth, brethren, that, if we are not of this world, we owe it not to ourselves, but to his special grace that has called us out of it; and this will keep us gentle, and tender, and lowly. But still, the fact remains the same, that just *on this very account*, the world hates us. The men of the world hate one another; amongst themselves, they are continually at variance. And yet they agree, with one mind, to hate those who are not of the world, but have been chosen out of it. But is there not even here something cheering, hopeful, and encouraging? The very hatred of the world should be to the Christian proof positive that he is not of the world, but has been drawn out of it.

This, then, is the explanation which Jesus gives of the world's hatred. And is there not something exceedingly solemn in the *frequency* with which Jesus uses the term 'world' in this connection? Not fewer than *six* different times does he use it in these two verses. Oh! ye who make light of being mere men of the world, see how Jesus looks at it in this context.

But further, our Lord next *reminds them of an important statement of his*, which they were never to forget: 'Remember the word that I said unto you, The servant is not greater than his lord.' They had already heard this saying three different times from his own blessed lips (Matt. 10:24; Luke 6:40; John 13:16). Here it is used in the same sense as in Matthew, but in a sense different from that in which it is used in John. There (in John 13:16) it is quoted as an encouragement to *humility*, but here as a motive to *patience* under persecution. 'If they have persecuted me, they will also persecute you.' Such is the connection between Christ and his people, that as the world dealt with him, so it would deal with them. The servants are not to be spared the pain of persecution, any more than their Master. And hence that cry, 'Saul, Saul, why persecutest thou me?' Yes, so long as the church militant shall last, the Apostle Paul's rule will hold good: 'All that will live godly in Christ Jesus *shall suffer persecution*.' And woe to the church whenever she loses the heavenly character of being hated and persecuted by a sinful world, until that day come, when the world shall lie down at her feet, bowing down before the sudden appearing of her glory. And then, as to the other words: 'If they have kept my saying, they will keep yours also,' they are not to be understood as introducing a new case; for the world, as such, did not keep his saying: but the meaning plainly is, my word and your word are so intimately joined that when you find the world, or any part of it, keeping my word, then, but not till then, may you expect them to keep yours. The one is just as unlikely, as impossible as the other.

[2] But further, our Lord now shows them that not only were they to suffer like their divine Master, but also

for his sake: 'But all these things will they do unto you for my name's sake' (verse :21). 'Nay, so far is this from being the case that you can be exempt from suffering, that it is just on this very account, *because* you belong to me, that you will be thus treated.'

And the *secret* of this opposition to Christ and to his people is thus explained: 'Because they know not him that sent me'—not they know not him as having sent me merely, but they know not *himself*. Ignorance of God—not desiring the knowledge of his ways—is the great secret of the world's hostility to Christ and his people. 'Oh, if they knew him that sent me, if they desired the knowledge of his ways, they would not treat me and my servants so; but they know him not. On the contrary, they hate God, and that hatred is the reason why they hate both me and mine.'

And the *sinfulness* of their conduct, the *aggravated* character of this sin, is also pointed out: 'If I had not come and spoken unto them, they had not had sin'— comparatively none, all other sins being light compared with the rejection of the Son of God—'but now,' says he, 'they have no cloak,' or pretext, 'for their sin.' Nay, their continued rejection of the Son of God, notwith-standing the palpable proofs which he had given them of his mission from the Father, stamped their charac-ter as one involving hatred of God: 'He that hateth me hateth my Father also' (verse 23). Hatred of him, who is the only manifestation of the Father to his creatures, amounted to hatred of the Father himself. Or, if the words of Jesus failed to have opened their eyes, surely his *works* ought to have done so: 'If I had not done among them the works which none other man did, they had not had sin' (verse 24). He refers to the testimony of his miracles; they had ocular demonstration of his divine mission; they were, therefore, altogether without excuse. Nay, in rejecting him, they gave evidence that they hated both him and the Father.

But all this treatment on the part of the world, however painful, was not to be wondered at; *it was only what was predicted in the Scripture*: 'But this cometh to pass,' says he, 'that the word might be fulfilled that is written in their law, They hated me without a cause.' We find the words both in Psalm 35:19 and 69:4; and they are here quoted by our Lord to show that when trials and persecutions for his name's sake should arise, they were not to be greatly surprised or discouraged, as though some strange thing had happened unto them, but rather to regard them as what they had every reason to expect.

It might now be a profitable and delightful exercise to turn our attention to the precious promise of the Comforter, with which Jesus seeks to cheer and strengthen their hearts, after this painful description of the world's hatred. But this subject, however inviting, must be postponed until a future occasion. Meanwhile let us learn from what has already been advanced.

In the first place, that *Christ and his people have the same enemies*. The human race is divided between two great potentates—the prince of light and the prince of darkness. Those who have been rescued from a state of nature are enlisted under the banner of the prince of light; but those who are still in their sins are enlisted under the banner of the prince of darkness. And the latter are here represented as arrayed in the most deadly hostility to Christ and his people. 'I will put enmity between thee and the woman, between thy seed and her seed,' are the words which the Lord spake unto the serpent immediately after the man fell (Gen. 3:15), and the history of the human race, from that day until now, is just an exemplification of them. Yea, it may be truly said that, as in the case of the divine Master, the more the glory of his Godhead shone forth, the more the enmity of the human heart was stirred against him, so also in the case of his disciples, the more they reflect the image of their Lord and Master, the more are they hated by an unbelieving world.

And therefore, observe here, secondly, that *the real source and secret of hatred to God's people is hatred to God himself.* 'But all these things will they do unto you for my name's sake, because they knew not him that sent me.' 'The carnal mind is enmity against God: for it is not subject to the law of God: neither indeed can be' (Rom. 8:7); and this enmity lies at the very root—it is the true explanation—of all the world's hatred of Christ and his people.

Further still, we learn here that *the rejection of the Son of God is the crowning evidence of the world's enmity to God.* 'If I had not come and spoken unto them, they had not had sin, but now they have no cloak for their sin.' And again, 'If I had not done among them the works which none other man did, they had not had sin; but now have they both seen and hated both me and my Father.' 'This is the condemnation, that light is come into the world, but men have loved darkness rather than the light.' Yes, the rejection of the Son of God is the most awful demonstration of the world's hatred of God!

But, finally, what a proof we have here of *the Redeemer's faithfulness and loving-kindness in thus warning his disciples of what they were to expect in the world*! How different is this from the way of the men of the world! If Jesus had been an imposter, he would have set a very different picture before them. But in faithfulness and tenderness, he tells them the worst of it. 'If any man will come after me, let him deny himself, and take up his cross and follow me.'

The Comforter Testifying
of Jesus

John 15:26–27

HAVING directed their attention to the painful
subject of the world's hatred, our Lord next, for
their encouragement, points them to the glorious Advocate, who was to conduct his cause and maintain it
triumphantly against an unbelieving world: 'But when
the Comforter is come whom I will send unto you from
the Father,' etc. He will afterwards refer more fully to
the gift and mission of the Comforter (16:5–15); but,
meanwhile, and before proceeding further, with this
most discouraging subject of which he has just been
speaking, he hastens to tell his disciples of that glorious
agent by whom they would prove victorious over the
world's opposition. Three properties, with this view,
does he ascribe to the blessed Comforter, which could
not fail to be exceedingly precious to their troubled
hearts.

First, he says that he would send him unto them
from the Father. He had already said that the Father

would give them another Comforter (14:16), that the Father would send him in his name (14:26); but here it is: 'Whom I will send unto you from the Father'—evidently implying that on his ascension to heaven, Christ as Mediator was to receive this gift from the Father, as the reward of his unfinished work. Accordingly, we read that when he ascended up on high, he received gifts for men (Psa. 68:18); and in like manner Peter said on the day of Pentecost, 'Therefore being by the right hand of God exalted, and having received of the Father the promise of the Holy Spirit, he hath shed forth this which ye now see and hear' (Acts 2:33). Yes, brethren, the enthroned Redeemer is concerned in the sending of the Comforter. He not only intercedes with the Father for the gift of the Spirit, but it is also one of his royal prerogatives to send him.

Secondly, our Lord *repeats* the Comforter's glorious title—'the Spirit of truth'—in opposition to the falsehood, the voluntary ignorance, and cruel hatred of the world. As the Spirit of truth, he would dissipate the darkness with which the world ever seeks to envelop itself. For he would lead them into the truth, which is essentially Christ himself (14:6); and in this strong tower they would be safely sheltered from the arrows of the wicked one; they would rise secure above the din and strife of the world.

And, thirdly, our Lord invites his disciples to cherish a joyful confidence in *the true divinity of the Spirit of truth*, 'who proceedeth from the Father.' It is hardly possible to refer these words to the same thing as is meant when it is said in the preceding clause, 'Whom *I will send* unto you *from the Father.*' For, besides that this would apparently be a mere repetition—mere tautology—the expression, 'I will send,' evidently refers to an historical event to take place at some future time; while the words, 'who proceedeth from the Father,' in the present tense, seem plainly to point to *a permanent, divine, and eternal relation.* And without adverting here, at any great length, to the ancient controversy, which rent asunder the Eastern and Western Churches, as to the *procession of the Holy Spirit*—the former Church maintaining that he proceeds from the Father *only*, and the latter, that he proceeds from the Father and also from the Son—I would only observe in passing that the offices of the three persons of the Godhead, in the scheme of grace, are founded on, and correspond to, their Trinitarian relations to one another. Indeed, the former would seem to be intended to be the reflection of the latter. The incarnation of the Son obviously corresponds to his eternal generation. And since it is affirmed here and elsewhere that the Holy Spirit is sent by the Son as well as by the Father, may we not from this infer, arguing from analogy that as the incarnation of the Son is related to his eternal generation from the Father, so is the mission of the Holy Spirit, in the plan of grace, to his eternal procession within the divine essence, from the *Son* as well as from the Father.

But without dwelling further on this controversy here, certain it is that our Lord's design in this whole description is to give his disciples the most exalted view of the Spirit's power and glory. The blessed Comforter that he was to send unto them from the Father, even the Spirit of truth, has a place within the undivided Godhead, and is therefore possessed of divine authority and power. This appears still more clearly from the emphatic use of that majestic word 'he'. It gathers up into one all the glorious qualities which have been ascribed to the Holy Spirit, and brings forth into view all the authority that belongs to him. 'He—this glorious Being, and only he,' our Lord would say, 'shall bear witness to, or testify of me, to the confusion of a sinful and persecuting world.'

In proceeding, therefore, to speak now of the *work* which is here ascribed to the divine Spirit, it may be observed that he had already testified of or borne witness to Christ, from the first gospel promise that sounded in the ears of sinners down to the last prophet, John the Baptist. Indeed, what is the whole of the Old Testament Scripture but one united testimony of the Holy Spirit concerning him that was to come? (1 Pet. 1:11–12; 2 Pet. 1:21). But he was soon to bear witness of him in a richer, fuller, and more glorious sense, than he had ever done before (John 7:39).

What then was this witness which the Holy Spirit was to bear of Jesus? It is certainly not to be referred to the *miracles* merely, that were wrought by the Holy

Spirit, in attestation of the divine mission of Jesus; for you will carefully observe that he is not merely speaking of some outward testimony borne in his favour, but of testimony borne to *himself*. Neither, on the other hand, is this witness to be confined to that which was borne in the *hearts* of the apostles. No doubt the Spirit testified of Jesus in their hearts; but it must not be limited to this, since the testimony spoken of was to be given *before the world*, and in condemnation of its hostile attitude. We conclude, therefore, that Jesus meant to speak of the witness that was to be borne by the *mouths* of the apostles, like that of Peter and the rest of the apostles on the day of Pentecost.

But if so—if by this testimony we are to understand that which was to be borne by the apostles—then why does he afterwards add: 'And ye also shall bear witness'? (verse 27). The answer to this question, I apprehend, is to be found in the words which follow: 'Because ye have been with me from the beginning.' The apostles are by no means to be regarded as mere passive instruments in the hand of the divine Spirit; on the contrary, they had a special testimony of their own to bear. They were chosen to be the constant companions of our Lord (Mark 3:14); and they were thus fitted to be the eye and ear witnesses of all that Jesus said and did (Luke 1:2). This was the reason why, when the apostles desired to fill up the place of Judas, they chose two men who had accompanied Jesus from the baptism of John to the day when Jesus 'was taken up'

(Acts 1:21, 22). Hence the testimony of the apostles and the testimony of the Spirit do not form *two separate* testimonies, but *one* and the *same*—having two sides upon it—a *divine* and a *human* side. The Apostle Peter specially refers to this distinction, when he says: 'And we are his witnesses of these things, and so is also the Holy Ghost' (Acts 5:32). The testimony of the apostles is, in one sense, *wholly divine*, and yet in another sense *wholly human*: so that while, on the one hand, the Holy Spirit watched over their discourse, guarded them against the possibility of error, purified, elevated, and strengthened their memories, each apostle, at the same time, speaks in his own peculiar way. Thus we recognise one and the same testimony to be both *divine* and *human*.

This, then, is the reason, why he mentions the witness of the Spirit and the witness of the apostles; it is but *two sides of the same testimony*. And this is *the great encouragement* that he holds out to them in view of the world's hatred. Is there not a lesson here for us? Are you hated, persecuted by the world? Does some trial oppress you, some deep sorrow wound you? Are you cast down, harassed because of sin within you and around you? How are you to rise superior to all this? Oh! I believe it is just in the very way that is here pointed out by our Lord—by the power of his Spirit and by the word of his testimony. For let us remember that while our position is unspeakably different from that of the apostles—while we are not the eye and the ear witnesses of what Jesus said and did—we have the *infallible* testimony of those who were, and the Spirit is graciously promised to lead us into the saving knowledge of the truth. Ah! yes, brethren, the blessed word which the inspired apostles have left us, and the gracious teaching of the promised Spirit, opening up our minds to perceive it, to realise it, and to receive it by faith—these are the two things that would raise us up superior to the world and its hatred.

And thus we, too, would become living witnesses for Jesus. For, when the Holy Spirit testifies of Christ by leading men to the saving knowledge of the truth, they also become so many living witnesses—so many reflecting lights, to shed forth the Saviour's glory—and this, just because they have been with him—not, indeed, in the outward literal sense, but in the higher, nobler sense of spiritual fellowship.

Finally, let us all remember the weighty words of the apostle that 'if any man'—high or low, rich or poor, young or old—'have not the Spirit of Christ'—whatever else he may have—'he is none of his.' And if not his, we know whose he is. Oh brethren, we must be Christ's or perish! We must receive him by faith, and give ourselves up to be his for ever. But Christ's we can never be without the Spirit's saving grace. May he now take of the things that are Christ's, and show them unto us!

The Disciples Persecuted
by the World

John 16:1–5

IN the commencement of this chapter, our Lord gives the reasons why he had said these things unto them. 'These things,' says he, 'have I spoken unto you'—'these things', including not only the warnings of the hatred of the world, but also the promise of the testifying Spirit—'these things have I spoken unto you, that ye should not be offended,' or rather 'stumble.' He desired indeed, on the one hand, that they should not be taken by surprise, when trials were actually encountered; but he desired also, on the other hand, that they might have, in the midst of their sufferings, some of his own words to remember, which would be the means of preserving them from fainting and unfaithfulness. What a dreary wilderness, what a dismal waste would this world be to the children of God, but for his own word of promise, which he has given them to lean upon!

But having thus encouraged his disciples, Jesus comes now to the most serious matter he has to communicate to them, concerning the subject of which he was speaking (15:18–25). Hitherto he had brought out especially the guilt of the persecutors; but now, in the present picture, he deals rather with the *sufferings of the persecuted*: 'They shall put you out of the synagogues.' But that is not the worst thing which you have to expect: 'Yea, the time cometh, that whosoever killeth you will think that he doeth God service' (verse 2). Oh! what blind infatuation is this! And it ought to be observed that the word rendered 'service' here means *religious* service—service specially rendered to God. The fanatical zeal of Saul of Tarsus, when he was consenting unto the death of Stephen (Acts 8:1), and when he 'went unto the high-priest, and desired of him letters to Damascus to the synagogues, that if he found any of this way, whether they were men or women, he might bring them bound unto Jerusalem' (Acts 9:1–2)—this fanatical zeal may be taken as a striking example of the state of mind described in verse 2. Ah! yes, a zeal for God may exist, which is not according to knowledge (Rom 10:2); and a man may be sincere, according to his natural light, in thinking that he is doing God service, while he is pursuing a course that leads him down to the chambers of death; yea, a blind zeal has often been observed to issue in the most inveterate opposition to Christ and his cause. But is it not the most infatuated blindness, is it not the deepest darkness to think to serve God by the very act which is an expression of the most vehement hatred against him?

But our Lord reveals again the *true secret* of this terrible opposition to himself and his cause: 'And these things will they do unto you, because they have not known the Father nor me' (verse 3). 'If they did, they would not so treat my disciples; but they do not know the Father nor me, and hence this bitter persecuting spirit.' The true explanation of hatred to God's people is hatred to God himself and his Christ; and there is not *a worse*, or a *more dangerous sign of ungodliness in any man, than hatred to God's people, and especially his public commissioned servants.*

But further, our Lord *explains again*, as in verse 1, *why he told them these things.* Oh! it was not because he had any pleasure in giving them pain—for 'he doth not afflict willingly, nor grieve the children of men'— but it was that, when the time of suffering should really come, they might remember that he told them of it (verse 4). For, however terrible their sufferings for Christ might be, the apostles by remembering his predictions, would no longer find in them a reason for doubt, but rather ground for faith and comfort. And, therefore, as he said in the case of Judas, 'Now I tell you before it come, that when it is come to pass, ye may believe that I am he' (13:19), so also he now forewarns them of their sufferings that they may have afterwards, in this very prediction, a ground of faith and comfort.

How touching moreover the reference to his not having told them these things before: 'And these things I said not unto you at the beginning, because I was with you' (verse 4)! So long as Jesus was with them, in his bodily presence, the blow was sure to fall upon himself; and therefore he spares their feelings by refraining from any allusion to the painful subject. But now he is about to leave them (verse 5); and consequently, in love and faithfulness, he will no longer conceal from them the dark future that lies before them.

On the whole, *what a melancholy picture we have here* (15:18–25; 16:1–5) *of our fallen human nature— of the unbelieving world—hating, persecuting the church of God!* Whence does this hostile, persecuting spirit proceed? From the enmity of the serpent's seed (Gen. 3:15); from human and Satanic agency; from the enmity of the carnal mind against God. But whatever be the source, various are the *forms* in which this spirit displays itself—ridicule, slander, disdain, cruel tortures, and the fiery furnace! Oh! what cause have we to bless God in these days for our civil and religious liberty! For if this persecuting spirit does not break out in our time, as in days gone by, in our own and in other lands, it is not because the unbelieving world is any better in itself, but it is because of *restraining grace and God's overruling providence.* Oh! surely the world needs to be converted—and must be converted ere it can even enter the kingdom. 'Whosoever hateth his brother is a murderer: and ye know that no murderer hath eternal life abiding in him' (1 John 3:15).

And is there not here also *a most important lesson for the true church of God—for the disciples of the*

Lord Jesus? Let them learn what they have a reason to expect in the world, and not be cast down or dismayed when trials come, as though something strange happened unto them. It is true indeed that some may try to escape persecution by being *unfaithful*; although usually such conduct is only followed by severer chastisements. And it is also true that sometimes men bring trials upon themselves by reckless and imprudent conduct; and indeed, we would always do well, when troubles arise, to enquire whether it is the cross of Christ we are bearing, or something else, which we may have brought upon ourselves by our unguarded conduct or lack of wisdom. Nevertheless, the divine rule holds good. 'Yea, and all that will live godly in Christ Jesus shall suffer persecution' (2 Tim. 3:12). Let a man endeavour, by the grace of God, to lead a holy life, and to lift up a testimony for Christ, and he will soon find, to his bitter cost, that the Cain-spirit is still alive on the earth. But what saith the Scripture for the comfort of such? 'Blessed are they who are persecuted for righteousness' sake: for theirs is the kingdom' (Matt. 5:10). And again: 'If ye be reproached for the name of Christ, happy are ye, for the Spirit of glory and of God resteth upon you—if any man suffer as a Christian let him not be ashamed; but let him glorify God on this behalf' (1 Peter 4:14, 16). Let us remember that these outward trials cannot injure the soul, that they last only for a time, and that they are working for us a far more exceeding and eternal weight of glory (2 Cor. 4:17).

And lastly, *what an affecting view have we here of the Lord Jesus, like a dying father in the midst of his children, comforting their hearts against the evils to come!* He withholds from them the painful prospect so long as he himself was among them; but now that he is about to leave them he will no longer conceal from them the dark future that lies before them. And yet even now he only discloses it that they might afterwards have another ground of faith and comfort, as they remembered his words. What exquisite tenderness was this! And let us remember that he is still the same tender, sympathising high priest—that his heart of love has undergone no change in its passage through death and the grave—that he has brought it up with him and sat down with it upon his throne: 'For we have not an high priest who cannot be touched with the feeling of our infirmities; but was in all points tempted as we are, yet without sin' (Heb. 4:15). Oh! it is indeed a blessed truth that there is a golden chain of holy, tender sympathy, stretching from the throne in glory, and reaching to the very humblest of his disciples on earth! He that said to Saul of Tarsus on the road to Damascus: 'Saul, Saul, why persecutest thou me?' (Acts 9:4), is still the same.

The Mission of the Comforter
and His Two-fold Work—
His Work on the World

John 16:5–15

IT is a dark, gloomy, and repulsive picture which Jesus sets before his disciples, of what they had reason to expect in the world. But having tenderly and faithfully warned them, he now proceeds, for their encouragement, to speak again—and in terms of greater clearness and fulness than before—of the mission of the Comforter, by whose blessed agency the world in arms against them was to be subdued (verses 5–11), and they themselves were to be fitted and furnished for their work (verses 12–15).

To this subject the reference to his own departure in verse 5, 'But now I go my way to him that sent me', forms the suitable introduction; for, while these words are a kind of natural sequel to those that immediately precede them, 'Because I was with you', they at the same time constitute the appropriate transition to the promise of the Paraclete—the ascension of the Redeemer to glory being the condition of the coming of the Spirit. Here, in this connection, our Lord tenderly complains: 'And none of you asketh me, Whither goest thou?' And yet indeed they had done so, after a sort, as manifested by the questions of Peter (13:36) and Thomas (14:5). But, besides that these questions related, the one to the possibility of following him, and the other to the difficulty of knowing the way, our Lord would evidently have them to be making more eager, intelligent, and joyful enquiry respecting *the nature* of an event which was to lead to such glorious results with regard both to him and to them. But instead of this, they dwelt so exclusively on the separation—on the dark side of the picture—that sorrow had filled their hearts: 'But because I have said these things unto you' (verse 6), that is to say, 'Because I have told you of parting, of conflict, and of suffering, sorrow hath filled your heart.' 'Nevertheless, notwithstanding,' continues the divine Redeemer, 'it is *expedient*—it is *advantageous* for you that I go away.' And oh! with what wonder must the disciples have listened to these words, and how anxiously must they have waited to hear the reason that could be given for so startling an intimation. Had they been left to their own reflections, and had they consulted together as to what would have been the severest trial they could be called to sustain—the heaviest blow which could be inflicted upon them—would they not with one consent have agreed in declaring that it would be the departure of their blessed Lord? 'Nevertheless,' says Jesus, 'it is expedient for you that I go away'—and expedient for this very reason, that 'if I go not away, the Comforter will not come unto you; but if I depart, I will send him unto you' (16:7).

When our Lord says here: 'If I go not away, the Comforter will not come unto you,' we are not to understand his words as if he meant to teach that heretofore the church was altogether destitute of the Spirit's grace, or that the disciples themselves, to whom he spake, had not experienced his saving power. On the contrary, we know, and are assured from many other passages of the divine word, that every soul that was ever saved from the days of Abel up to the present hour, was so—was enlightened, quickened, sanctified, and comforted—by his spiritual power. But, on the other hand, it is certainly implied in these words that the Holy Spirit was to be poured out in larger measure, and in more copious showers, after the ascension of our Redeemer, than he had ever been before. And if I were asked, why? Why was the Holy Spirit to be poured out in richer abundance now than before? I would say it was to be *the crowning evidence—the peculiar and appropriate proof*—of the completion of his work, of its acceptance in the court of heaven, and of the glory to which he was in consequence raised. This I take to be part at least of Peter's meaning on the day of Pentecost, when he said: 'Therefore being by the right hand of God exalted, and having received of the Father the promise of the Spirit, he hath shed forth this, which ye now see and hear' (Acts 2:33). It would seem as if God intended to show the glory to which his Son was raised by pouring out his Spirit in larger measure and in richer abundance than he had ever done before.

But what I wish you specially to notice here is *the unspeakable importance which our Lord attaches to the gift and mission of the Comforter*: 'It is *expedient* for you', says he, 'that I go away.' If it was expedient for them that he should go away in order that the Comforter might come, does this not imply that the Spirit's advent would *compensate*, ay, and *more than compensate*, the church for any loss she might sustain from the want of the Saviour's bodily presence? Ah! it would be well for us to remember this lesson. We sometimes hear men say, or if they do not say it in so many words, they think it in their hearts—that if they had lived in the Saviour's day, if they had been permitted to hear his voice and to witness his miracles, it would be better with them than it is. And yet the very lesson which Jesus here teaches his chosen disciples, 'that companied with him' for years, is that their future condition would *not* be worse, but *better* when he should leave them, because then the Holy Spirit would descend. But how is this? How is the Spirit's coming of more importance than the Saviour's visible presence? The Holy Spirit is the great applier of Christ and of his benefits to the souls of men. But besides this, it was impossible, in the nature of things, that Christ's bodily presence and agency could be enjoyed in more than one place at more than one time; it was confined to the narrow limits of the land Judaea, whereas the presence and power of the divine Spirit knows no geographical bounds; it is to be enjoyed everywhere and at all times. And hence the gospel-dispensation—the dispensation of the Spirit under which we live—is *worldwide*: 'Go ye into all the world, and preach the gospel to every creature.'

Let us now proceed to consider the comprehensive statement which our Lord makes regarding the nature and design of the Spirit's work. It is represented as consisting of *two* great parts, and as designed for two widely different classes of men—the world and the church (verses 8–15).

With reference to the first part of his work—and it is to this only that we can now advert—it is said: 'And when he is come, he will reprove the world of sin, and of righteousness, and of judgment,' etc. (verses 8–11). In proceeding to open up the meaning of these words, it may be observed that the best commentary on them is the day of Pentecost with its glorious results, as recorded in the second chapter of the Acts; and along with this, a man's own experience of the Spirit's work. It is remarkable that the apostles, the instruments of the Spirit's agency, are not once named here; they disappear entirely out of view in the glory of the divine being who works through their instrumentality: 'And *he*, when he is come,' etc. With regard to the word which is here rendered 'reprove,' it may be remarked, that it has no exact synonym in our language, and it is exceedingly difficult to find one term sufficient to express its profound significance. The word 'reprove' is certainly far too weak, inasmuch as it gives you the idea merely of an outward rebuke; whereas the word here used denotes something which reaches the heart and conscience. There is no reason, however, why we should be in any doubt as to the real meaning of the word. It signifies to *convict*, or *convince by proof of a fault or error*—to refute an error. Yes, the Spirit's testimony to an unbelieving world partakes largely of the character of a conviction, or a refutation of an error. The world is at fault, or in error with regard to three different things—sin, righteousness, and judgment. It is the Spirit's work to convict the world of its fault—to refute its error with regard to these things; or, in other words, to present such evidence of its fault or error as will be sufficient to condemn, if it fail to convince. The three great subjects with respect to which the Spirit is to convict the world of its fault or error are put before us, in the first instance, in the most indefinite manner—'sin, righteousness, and judgment'; but they are afterwards defined by qualifying clauses: of sin, *because they believe not on me*; of righteousness, *because I go unto the Father, and ye see me no more*; and of judgment, *because the prince of this world is judged*. Let us now consider each of these three things in their order.

[1] And first with regard to *sin*. When carnal men— when mere men of the world—talk of sin, I suppose

they generally mean shameful crimes or gross violations of the divine law; but when the Holy Spirit comes to convict of sin, he reveals to men another sin, of which naturally they think nothing—viz., that of *not believing in Jesus*. As all sin has its root in unbelief in the heart (Psa. 14:1), so the most aggravated form of unbelief is the rejection of the Son of God. Jesus is the supreme good; to reject him, therefore, is the crowning evil. It is the Spirit's work to convict the world of its terrible fault or error in this matter. This he did, by the mouth of Peter, on the day of Pentecost; and this he still does through the instrumentality of his commissioned servants. In fastening this charge—the charge of unbelief—on the conscience, however, the Holy Spirit does not extinguish, but rather deepens and intensifies the sense of all other sins. Oh! brethren, have we been convicted by the Spirit of God of our great fault and error in the rejection of the Son of God?

[2] But, secondly, if the world is at fault or in error on the subject of sin, it is certainly not the less so, with regard to *righteousness*. The world—the unbelieving world—in its false ideas of righteousness, condemned as a malefactor the Lord of glory. When the Holy Spirit comes, he teaches men what righteousness really is, by bringing home the truth to the heart and conscience, that he, whom the world condemned as a malefactor, is now exalted to the right hand of God: 'Of righteousness, because I go to the Father, and ye see me no more.' In this respect, the Holy Spirit acts the part of

an infallible judge; and his verdict is that it was those who condemned him that were the malefactors, and that it was he that was condemned that was the Righteous One. This meaning appears to me to arise most fairly (1) in the first instance, from the *contrast* between the terms *sin* and *righteousness*; and just as they that believed not are, at the same time, the very persons to whom sin belongs, so, on the other hand, he who is gone to the Father is the very same to whom righteousness belongs. But (2) the same thing appears still more clearly from *the fact that the same term—convict—is applied to righteousness as to sin.* For it will never do to attach one meaning to the word when we speak of sin, and another, when we speak of righteousness; and it will hardly do to speak of convicting men of the justifying righteousness of Christ. But no language could be more appropriate if we understand our Lord's words as meaning that when the Spirit comes, he will convict men of their great fault in the matter of righteousness, by bringing home the truth that he, whom they crucified as a malefactor, is now glorified at the right hand of God. Plainly therefore, by the term righteousness here, we are to understand Christ's *personal* righteousness, or the rectitude of his divine claims. Most unquestionably, this is the light in which the subject was presented by Peter on the day of Pentecost, when he said: 'Therefore let all the house of Israel know assuredly, that God hath made that same Jesus whom ye have crucified both Lord and Christ' (Acts 2:36). Ye have crucified him, but God hath made him both Lord and Christ (compare also Acts 3:14–15; 4:10). And it is very remarkable that it was just when he had pressed home this truth that 'they were pricked in their hearts, and said unto Peter and the rest of the apostles, Men and brethren, what shall we do?' And no wonder, though they should thus cry out; for if God had made him both Lord and Christ, whom they had crucified, then they were guilty of fighting against God; and then, too, they were in *danger*; for all power in heaven and on earth was put into his hands. And when we, too, shall believe that he, whom we have so often rejected, is now both Lord and Christ, like them we shall cry: 'What shall we do?'

[3] If there is sin, on the one hand, and righteousness on the other, there must also be *judgment*. And springing from a principle of righteousness, it would seem that this judgment must strike at the unbelieving sinner just spoken of. But no; it is not so; the judgment of which the Holy Spirit is to give the world a demonstration is not that of the world *itself*—for the world may and will, through grace, be saved, if it yields to the reproofs of mercy—but it is the judgment of 'the prince of this world.' 'Of judgment, because the prince of this world is judged' (verse 11). But how is this? How is the prince of this world judged? Take the answer in the following way: Satan claimed the world as his own—to be its rightful owner. But in the cross of Christ that claim has been set aside at once and for ever. It is true, indeed, that Satan did bruise Messiah's heel; but he who

was David's Lord as well as David's son bruised Satan's head (Gen. 3:15); and having spoiled principalities and powers, he made a show of them openly, triumphing over them in his cross (Col. 2:15). From that hour Satan has been actually judged—*condemned to be cast out* (12:31–32). His ancient kingdom has been opened up for the promulgation of the everlasting gospel; and by the Spirit's mighty working in the hearts of men, Satan is *actually cast out*, and the soul rescued from his grasp. 'Shall the prey be taken from the mighty, or the lawful captive be delivered? But thus saith the Lord, Even the captives of the mighty shall be taken away, and the prey of the terrible shall be delivered' (Isa. 49:24–25). So that every sinner snatched from Satan's chains and truly regenerated by the Spirit is a living witness of the sentence passed upon, and the victory obtained over him, who was once the prince of this world.

Thus, then, does the Spirit convict the world of sin, of righteousness, and of judgment. And you observe that the three great subjects on which he is to shed a clear and convincing light have all of them a reference to Christ. Does he convince of sin? It is because they believe not on Jesus. Does he convict the world of its great fault in the matter of righteousness? It is by bringing home the truth that he, who was condemned as a malefactor, is now gone to the Father. And finally, does he convince the world of judgment? It is because, in the cross of Christ, the prince of this world is judged—condemned.

But the question is, What is to be the effect of this work of the Spirit? Alas! some may still remain under the power of unbelief, and so share the judgment of the prince of this world; for conviction does not always issue in conversion. But in the case of others, this teaching, by the blessing of God will have a very different effect, translating them from darkness to light and from the kingdom of Satan to the kingdom of God's dear Son. But if this glorious result is to be produced through the instrumentality of the apostles, his work must be done *in themselves.* And accordingly you will observe that our Lord now passes from the Spirit's work upon the world *by* believers to his work *in* them. For let us ever remember that, when the Lord is about to bless the world, it is his usual way first to bless the church.

Meanwhile, it is of infinite importance for us to ask, How stands the matter with us? I believe that the Spirit of God has often been striving with each one of us, and perhaps with some of you since you now entered this house. What is to be the result of it? Oh! remember that the gospel of Christ must be to each of us either the savour of life unto life, or the savour of death unto death. Grieve not the Spirit; quench not the Spirit; resist not the Holy Ghost.

The Mission of the Comforter—
His Work in the Church

John 16:12–15

IT is a characteristic of our Lord's farewell discourse
to his disciples that in it he went more fully into the
office and work of the Holy Spirit than at any previous
period of his ministry. Not fewer than four different
times, within the compass of a few verses, does he refer
to the gift and mission of the Comforter, as being of
unspeakable importance to the church of God (14:16–
17, 26; 15:26; 16:7–11). In two of these passages he
speaks of the Holy Spirit as given or sent by the Father
in his name and on the ground of his finished work and
intercession; and in the other two, he promises that he
himself would send him, as having received that gift
from the Father. In the verses immediately preceding,
he plainly intimates that the gift of the Holy Spirit
would compensate, ay, and more than compensate the
church for any loss that it might sustain from the want
of his bodily presence. And then, in a few great strokes,
he depicts all and every part of the Spirit's work—his

work on the world and in the church. Having already spoken somewhat of the first of these, I come now to consider his work in the church.

Here he begins by showing them *the necessity* of the Spirit's teaching. 'I have yet many things to say unto you, but ye cannot bear them now' (verse 12). Notwithstanding all the instructions that he had given them, he still had many things to say to them, but they were not in a condition to hear them yet. Most assuredly he had kept nothing back from them from want of love to them (15:15); but because of their want of capacity to receive them, he had kept to himself many revelations which were reserved for the Spirit's teaching. These 'many things'—these higher revelations—comprise all in the writings of the apostles, which goes beyond the words of Christ in the Gospels. Indeed, in some respects, the teaching of Jesus had but sown the seeds, which the Spirit came to fructify.

But then referring to the Spirit's teaching, he says: 'Howbeit when he, the Spirit of truth is come, he will guide you into all truth' (verse 13). Notice again the all-important title, which he gives the Holy Spirit: 'The Spirit of truth.' And as is the title, such is the work: 'He will guide you into all truth'—literally, 'He will show you the road into all truth.' In this significant expression, the Holy Spirit is represented under the figure of a leader, conducting a traveller into an unknown country. That country is truth. I need hardly say that by the phrase 'all truth' here we are to understand 'all truth' bearing on faith and practice—on the glory of God and the salvation of men—all revealed truth. Into this truth the Holy Spirit would guide them clearly, plainly, and powerfully. And further, when it is said: 'into all truth,' his words imply the *completeness and perfection* of the word of God—that no new word of Christ shall ever be added thereto—and consequently, the vanity of looking for any new revelations of the Spirit, beyond what we have in the written word.

And, then, *the divine authority, the infallibility* of this guide, arises from the same cause as that of Jesus himself (7:17–18): 'He shall not speak of himself,' that is, from himself, 'but whatsoever he shall hear, that shall he speak' (16:13). But hear of whom? Of the Father and the Son. The next verses prove that these two ideas must be combined; and this most naturally explains the expression: 'Whatsoever he shall hear.' In other words, he is conversant with the special communications between the Father and the Son; he knows all their divine counsels; and being accessory to all these, he instructs his disciples according to their need. In this connection, it is further promised: 'And he will show you things to come'—referring especially to the revelations, which in the Epistles, partially, but most fully, in the Apocalypse, open up a vista into the future kingdom—the revelation of the future destiny of the church—'the things to come' (Rev. 1:1). Observe here, in passing, how complete the evidence of the inspiration of the New Testament Scriptures. The New Testament consists partly of a narrative; and in this respect the Spirit is promised in these terms: 'He shall teach you all things, and bring all things to your remembrance whatsoever I have said unto you' (14:26). It is partly doctrinal, and the Spirit is promised in these terms: 'He shall guide you into all truth.' It is partly prophetical, and the Spirit is promised in these words: 'He will show you things to come.' Or, to put the case more succinctly still, the formula of the inspiration of the Gospels is: 'He shall teach you all things, and bring all things to your remembrance.' And the formula of the inspiration of the Epistles and Apocalypse is: 'He shall guide you into all truth; and 'He shall show you things to come.' Thus the proof of the inspiration of the New Testament is complete; and when once we have reached this point, the inspiration of the Old Testament immediately follows; for every book in the Old Testament is quoted, or referred to, in the New Testament as one of divine authority, and with divine approbation.

But *what is the end and aim of the Spirit's work in the revelation of the truth?* 'He shall glorify me; for he shall receive of mine, and shall show it unto you' (verse 14). He has just been speaking of his guiding them into all truth, and then, without a break in the connection, he adds: 'He shall glorify me.' Does not the close relation between verse 14 and what precedes show us that the whole design of the Holy Spirit in the revelation of the truth is nothing else but the glorifying of Christ in the hearts of the apostles, and by their means, in the hearts of all believers? Christ—in his person, and work, and love—this is the only text on which the Holy Spirit will shed a glorious light in the souls of the disciples. Let us, therefore, consider here, first, *the nature and character of the Spirit's work*, as pointed out in the words: 'He shall glorify me'; and then, secondly, *the significant explanation*, which our Lord subjoins, as to *the way* and *manner* in which the Spirit executes the work: 'for he shall receive of mine and show it unto you.'

[1] And first, *the nature and character* of the Spirit's work as brought before us in the words: 'He shall glorify me.' There was a time indeed, when he said: 'I have glorified thee,' but now he says: 'He shall glorify me.' And what is the inference so fairly deducible from a comparison of these two texts? It was the delight of the Son to glorify the Father; it is the delight of the Spirit to glorify the Son. Not that the Holy Spirit adds anything to the *personal* and *mediatorial* glories which now encircle him as seated on the throne of his glory; for in that respect nothing was left undone by the Father, when he raised him from the dead and set him at his own right hand. But the Holy Spirit glorifies Jesus *in the view and experience of men*. Indeed, it is truly delightful to notice the different instances of *glorifying* that we have here. The Son glorified the Father *on earth*; the Father glorified the Son *in heaven* (17:4–5); and now again the Holy Spirit glorifies Jesus *on the earth, in the hearts of his people*. Let us consider briefly how he does it.

And here I must not forget that the first step which he takes is *to lay the sinner low and prostrate in the dust.* For in what does the Spirit's preparation consist? Not in bettering the sinner's condition in his own experience, but in making it worse. He humbles and uncrowns the pride of self before he glorifies Jesus. He awakens grief, which none but Jesus can assuage; he inflicts a wound, which none but Jesus can heal; he creates a void in the soul, which none but Jesus can fill up; in a word, he brings the sinner to such a case that none but Jesus can meet the condition of his soul. 'They that be whole need not a physician, but they that are sick.'

But then, having prepared the soul for the blessing, by revealing its poverty of state and producing real poverty of spirit, the Holy Spirit next proceeds to glorify the Saviour, *by showing how suitable a Saviour Jesus is to meet the case of such a soul*—that he is an all-sufficient Saviour—almighty to save unto the uttermost all that come unto God through him, and as willing as he is able. Oh! what a glorifying of Jesus is this, when the Spirit of God opens the blind eye to see the glory, all-sufficiency, and suitableness of Christ as a Saviour. All that the poor sinner needs he now finds in Jesus—a righteousness to meet the claims of God's law and justice, before which he was utterly helpless—a covert to shield him from all the terrors of the divine wrath—a supply for all his wants—a cure for all his diseases—and a deliverance from all his enemies. Oh! it is a strange wondering that this new light produces in his soul. It is impossible that this divine knowledge can be imparted without the result being that all on which he looked before as a ground of hope has been utterly eclipsed in his view; and his one desire now is to be found in Christ, not having his own righteousness, but that which is through the faith of Christ (Phil. 3:3–9).

And therefore I remark further, the Holy Spirit glorifies Christ *by causing the soul to give him his own place on the throne of the renewed heart and will*. For in the day that he opens the blind eye to see his glory, he opens the closed heart to receive him. 'Thy people shall be willing in the day of thy power.' Oh! what a hearty welcome does the soul now give to Christ, when the will is renewed. 'Lift up your heads, ye gates, and be ye lifted up ye everlasting doors.' 'Blessed is he that cometh in the name of the Lord.' Verily, in the sinner's view, and in his *heart* also, Christ has the pre-eminence. Oh! how sweet it is now to rest on his person, righteousness, and grace, and to be unreserved in devoting heart and soul to his blessed service.

By enabling the believer to lead a progressive life of faith, the Holy Spirit glorifies Jesus. He does not allow the subject of his saving grace to rest on his own work in him, but he keeps him consciously 'poor and needy,' that he may be dependent on Christ for all he needs. Just as the famished multitudes in Egypt were all dependent on Joseph, so the child of God is kept dependent on the New Testament Joseph for all he needs. Oh! how this tends to the glorifying of Christ, when the soul, in conscious emptiness, is kept constantly hanging on divine fulness. What a proof is thus furnished of the power, faithfulness, and loving kindness of the Saviour!

And surely, the Holy Spirit glorifies Christ *by transforming the soul into his divine image.* 'Beholding as in a glass the glory of the Lord, we are changed into the same image, from glory to glory, even as by the Spirit of the Lord' (2 Cor. 3:18). This is the goal on which the eye is set; this is the standard, to which he desires to be conformed—even the perfect image of Christ; and it is just as he unveils his eye before the glory of Christ that he is changed into the very same image.

Further still, the Holy Spirit glorifies Jesus *by enabling his people to render active service,* and, perhaps, also *to suffer for his sake.* He does not take the man who is the subject of his saving grace altogether aside from the world, to spend his life in a cloister. Seasons for private meditation and prayer—quiet Sabbaths during his life—there are, and there must be, as there were in the life of the man Christ Jesus himself; but even these are fitted and intended to prepare him for further service. True indeed, there are some who are shut up, in the providence of God, in retirement, so that they can only serve him in secret, and glorify him by suffering meekly for his sake. But these do indeed serve the Lord, and not only does he accept the work, but the church of God is much benefited thereby. Secret wrestlers with God are an unspeakably precious treasure;

and it is just in proportion as we have these amongst us that the church has real power with God.

And the result of the whole of the Spirit's work in the church is that she is made glorious, that he, in the last day, 'may be glorified in his saints, and admired in all them that believe.'

[2] But I come now in the second place, to consider *the significant explanation* which our Lord gives, as to *the way* in which the Spirit executes this work: 'For he shall receive of mine and show it unto you.' What, then, are the things of Christ, of which the Spirit takes? How does he take of them? And how does he show them unto us? These are the three questions which here present themselves for solution.

1. What are the things of Christ, of which the Holy Spirit is to receive? He himself tells us in the verse immediately following: 'All things that the Father hath are mine.' This most wonderful saying reveals, as none other does, the consciousness that he possessed of his greatness, and riches, and glory. A plainer expression than this of absolute equality, and community of interest, with the Father, cannot well be conceived. Oh! where is the mere creature on earth, or the angel in heaven that could adopt such language as this—that could say: 'All that the Father hath is mine'? But Jesus could say it, and it is just because he could, that he said, 'he shall take of mine.' 'Therefore'—on this ground— 'said I that he shall take of mine.' The meaning is that it was on the ground of his being able to claim all that the

Father has as his own that he could say: 'he shall take of mine.'

What, then, are the things that the Father has? Whatsoever they are, Jesus has them, and to these he refers, when he says: 'he shall receive of mine.' All that the Father has, *as God*, is his. There is not a perfection of the divine nature, natural or moral, that is not the Son's, as surely as it is the Father's. 'I and the Father are one,' says he; and he also declares: 'He that hath seen me hath seen the Father.' All that the Father has *as righteousness* to justify the sinner, Christ has. He it was that assumed our nature, in order to work it out; he it was that wrought out and brought in an everlasting righteousness. All that the Father has *as the provision of his love* for his people, Christ has; for 'it pleased the Father that in him should all fulness dwell.' It is all the Father's provision—the provision of his love and wisdom, and yet it is all laid up in Christ, to be dispensed by him to 'the poor and needy.'

Now these divine riches of Christ, in common with the Father, are those of which the Spirit takes. There can be no revelation of the divine glory, or of the righteousness of God, or of the grace of the everlasting covenant, which is not a manifestation of what is Christ's. The unsearchable riches of divine glory, of divine merit, and of divine grace—ah! these are the very things with which it would be well to become acquainted; and these are the very things of which the Holy Spirit receives, in order to show them to his people.

2. But secondly, *how does the Holy Spirit receive*, or rather, *take them* as in verse 15? The original word is capable of both renderings, and we may think of him as receiving from the Father and the Son, or we may think of him as taking them in the exercise of his own love and sovereignty. But as the scope of the whole passage is simply to bring out the Spirit's work with relation to Christ, it is far better to understand the word as meaning—'He shall *take* of mine;' that is, he shall take freely, and in the exercise of his own love and sovereignty. Observe, my friends, the order in which these things are put down: (1) 'All things that the Father hath;' (2) 'All things that the Father hath *are mine*;' and therefore (3) 'He shall take of mine.' The offices of the three Persons of the Godhead are founded on their personal relations to one another; or, in other words, according to the order of their subsistence in the Godhead is the order of their operation in the economy of grace. It was the Father's work to plan, to purpose; it was the Son's place to purchase; and now it was the Spirit's work, in the exercise of the same love and sovereignty, to apply the purchased redemption.

Nor is it too minute to observe that there is more documentary evidence for the present time—'takes'—than for the future—'will take.' It is besides more in harmony with what is said of the Father and the Son: All that the Father *hath*; and again, *'are* mine.' 'He takes;' that is to say, this is his constant, permanent work. 'All things that the Father *hath are* mine'; therefore he *taketh* of mine.

3. But if the Spirit takes of the things that are Christ's, it is in order *to show them to his people.* There was a time indeed in my life when I would have thought that these words would have read better thus: 'And *give* them unto you.' But now I see that they are infinitely better as they are; since it is the design of the Spirit's work *not* to make the believer the *depository* of his own grace, but *to point him to, and to keep him dependent on, him in whom all fulness dwells.*

But, perhaps, the first thing that we are led to think of here is *the external revelation of the things of Christ contained in the divine record.* True indeed, he was pleased to make use of *human instruments*; and we rejoice in the visible prints of human authorship; they make the book far more human, and far better adapted to us. But while he was pleased to make use of these, yet the Spirit of God is, in the fullest sense, the *divine author.* 'Holy men of God spake as they were moved by the Holy Ghost.' He regulated and controlled, without in the least modifying the mental peculiarities of the men whom he used in the work. Surely we need not be surprised at this combination of the human with the divine in the work of producing the record, when we think how they were united in the work of redemption, and how they are still united in the work of grace and providence. And surely it was to be expected that when God was giving to his church and bride a revelation of himself, of his mind and will, it would be, in every respect, worthy of himself. Yes, the Holy Spirit has shown the things of Christ in the Bible; and his work in doing so is, like himself, absolutely perfect.

But there is also *an internal revelation* of the things of Christ, by means of the word in the soul. 'The natural man receiveth not the things of the Spirit of God' (1 Cor. 2:14). The things of Christ are revealed in the book, and they are there in order to be known of us. But known of us *they never will be, unless the Spirit reveals them*. 'Blessed art thou, Simon Bar-Jona, for flesh and blood hath not revealed this unto thee, but my Father, who is in heaven.' Yes, it is the Spirit's work to take them as they are in the book, and reveal them *inwardly* to us. In doing this, *he enables the soul to perceive their excellence and glory*, so that it can never be at rest without them. Ay, and he shows them the things of Christ in such a way as *to help them to exercise an appropriating faith*; for it is not his way to tantalise the soul by holding out to it what it is never to partake of; nay, but he enables the soul, under a sense of its own emptiness, to appropriate from day to day the fullness that is in Jesus. And the effect of such a revelation as this is *a transformation into the divine image.*

Thus it is that the Holy Spirit takes of the things that are Christ's, and shows them unto us, in his own clear, powerful, and affecting light. And thus it is that he glorifies Jesus—makes him glorious in the estimation and experience of his people.

And now in closing, we may use this text, first, as a *test*. There are a thousand things in the world that claim to be of the Spirit of God. There are *doctrines*, there are *ministries*, and there are *experiences*, that claim to be of God. The single test that we would apply to them all is, Whither do they lead? Do they tend to honour and exalt the Saviour? Whatsoever is of the Spirit of God tends to glorify Jesus. But more especially would we apply this test here to Christian experience. We sometimes hear men ask, How shall I know whether I am under the teaching of the Spirit of God? whether I am under the influence of the Spirit or the flesh? Whither does that teaching, or that influence lead you? Is it to Christ? Then it is of the Spirit of God. There is not, there cannot be, a clearer evidence that a man is under the teaching that is from above than this, that he is led to Christ, and that he seeks to put the crown of his salvation on his blessed head.

Secondly, this text *leaves all who do not esteem Christ as the pearl of great price, utterly excuse-less.* For, think you, could not he, whose office it is to glorify Jesus, bring even you to know him, to love him, and to serve him? And yet you may have never sought his help. This of itself is sufficient to leave you without excuse. Oh, fall in, soul, with the Spirit's way! It is his delight to honour the Saviour. Be it yours to fall in with the Spirit's way.

Finally, this text is *full of comfort to all who would fain honour and love the Saviour.* Ah! well did Jesus know what suits the felt wants and living desires of his own. He knew that they would feel—keenly feel—their want of esteem for him; and that love to him would earnestly long for the day when he would be glorified *in* them and *by* them; yea, for the day when he would be glorified in all men, from the rising to the setting sun. See how he meets the cravings of the renewed heart in the promise of the text! Truly this is spiritual drink—living water—that satisfies the thirst of all the friends and lovers of Jesus: 'He shall glorify me, for he taketh of mine, and shall show it unto you.'

[C]

Conclusion of the Discourse

John 16:16–33

Two Little Whiles—
Sorrow Turned into Joy

John 16:16–24

O UR Lord's discourse is now drawing nigh to a close. He has set before the disciples some most important truths respecting their position in the world. He has shown them their proper relations to himself, and to one another; he has warned them of the world's hatred and opposition; and he has held out glorious encouragements to them in the promise of the Comforter. And now, as is most natural, he returns from these different subjects to that one great event which so engrossed the present moment—his approaching departure—when the conversational or dialogue form again appears (verses 17, 29).

In attempting to explain the enigmatical saying, the apparently contradictory statement: 'A little while, and ye shall not see me: and again, a little while, and ye shall see me,' it ought to be mentioned that we have not in the original the same word for 'seeing' in both cases; on the contrary, two different words are used—the first referring to physical sight merely, but the second to spiritual sight as well. What, then, are we to make of these two little whiles? If the seeing promised at the end of the second refers to the appearances of Jesus after his resurrection, as some maintain, then there is no connection between verse 16 and the preceding context. But it is very clear that there is a very deep and close connection between them. Jesus has been speaking of his Spirit guiding them into all truth, and of his being glorified by his Spirit in the hearts of his people; and then, without a break in the sequence, he speaks of their seeing him again. Does not this prove that the seeing refers to the illumination of the Spirit at Pentecost? And besides this, the same thing appears from the *reason given*: 'Because I go to the Father.' What was Jesus to do when he should go to the Father? He was to send the Comforter. When, therefore, it is said that they were to see him again, because he was to go to the Father, we have every reason to believe that the seeing promised is the seeing of faith by the power of the Holy Spirit. Clearly then, the first 'little while' is that which came to an end at the death of Jesus, when he in a manner disappeared from *outward* view; but the second 'little while' is that which ended at Pentecost, when the Spirit was poured out from on high. It is true indeed that Jesus appeared often to his disciples after his resurrection; and that 'to all that look for him, he shall appear the second time without sin unto salvation'; but it is also true that the great central truth to which our attention is here pointed is their seeing him by faith after the out-pouring of the Spirit at Pentecost; for which indeed the appearances after the resurrection prepared the way; even as this believing view of him prepares the soul for his appearance at the last day, which will be the final consummation, the glorious completion of the whole (14:19–21).

And there is every reason to believe that our Lord *purposely* expressed himself in this enigmatical way in order to stimulate enquiry, and to draw forth from them an acknowledgment of their doubts and difficulties. In point of fact we have here just another instance of that peculiar mode of instruction by dark sayings, sometimes adopted by our Lord, and of which we have already had a sample or two in chapter 14:4–7. By such paradoxical statements our Lord designed to elicit from them an honest confession of their difficulties, in order that he himself might take them out of the way for ever.

At all events, his words had this effect on the disciples; they are perplexed and bewildered; and in their bewilderment 'some of them said among themselves, What is this that he saith unto us?' etc. (verses 17, 18). Philip would ask Andrew, and Peter would turn enquiringly to John and say, 'What is this that he saith unto us?' Two things, especially, seemed most mysterious unto them—these two short delays, which were to be followed by such opposite results, and then that apparently contradictory notion: 'Ye shall see me, because I go away'—these things are perfect enigmas to them;

they cannot understand them. And no wonder; for, however clear these words may now be to us, looking back upon them as past and accomplished, they must have been most mysterious to them. Ah! yes, brethren, there are many things in the Lord's dealings with 'his own', by his word and in his providence, which are very dark and perplexing to them now; they cannot for the present understand them.

But he who, from the very outset, only designed to elicit their inquiries, *now sees what was passing through their minds, and proceeds to remove their difficulties*: 'Now Jesus knew that they were desirous to ask him, and said unto them, Do ye enquire among yourselves of that I said, A little while, and ye shall not see me: and again, a little while, and ye shall see me?' (verse 19)—repeating the very words which seemed so strange to them. And then with his solemn 'Verily, verily,' by which he ever seeks to find an entrance for his truth into their hearts, he goes on to unravel the mystery: 'Verily, I say unto you, That ye shall weep and lament, but the world shall rejoice: and ye shall be sorrowful, but your sorrow shall be turned into joy' (verse 20).

In these words Jesus gives them another and most convincing proof of his divine knowledge, not only by letting them see that he was perfectly acquainted with all the questions which were now occupying their minds, but also and especially, by solving all the dark mysteries by which they were perplexed. And yet instead of giving them an *outward revelation* of those great events which were so soon to take place—which indeed they do not seem as yet to be in a capacity to receive—he only describes the *inward impressions* of which they were to be themselves the subjects. And between these impressions and the two little whiles, there was to be the closest relation; corresponding to the little while, at the expiry of which, they were *not* to see him, they were to *weep and lament*; but corresponding to the second 'little while,' at the end of which they were to see him, *their sorrow would be turned into joy.*

Observe, my friends, the *double* contrast—the contrast between *the church* and *the world*, and the contrast between the church's *past sorrows* and *future joys*.

In the first instance, there is a contrast between *the disciples and the world*: 'Ye—my disciples—shall weep and lament, but the world shall rejoice' (verse 20). As Christ's disciples, as God's church, they were to weep and lament; whilst the world, the foe of Jesus, would triumphantly rejoice. These tears and lamentations of the disciples find their explanation in the tears of Mary Magdalene (chapter 20), and in the state of the disciples generally after their Master's death; while the joy of the world found its first expression in the scoffs and sneers of the passers-by at the crucifixion. And in like manner, what causes the church of God the deepest sorrow—what is as a sword in their bones—is turned by the world into an occasion of rejoicing and merriment.

But secondly, if there is a contrast between the church and the world, there is also a contrast between *the church's past sorrows and future joys*: 'And ye shall be sorrowful, but your sorrow shall be turned into joy.' This is indeed the main idea—the other being only a kind of inserted parenthetic contrast by the way. And therefore our Lord reproduces the idea of sorrow: 'And ye shall be sorrowful,' in order to bring out the more vividly the originally intended contrast: 'But your sorrow shall be turned into joy.' No doubt this was partially fulfilled at the resurrection; but perfect joy was not restored till the day of Pentecost. And observe you the peculiar strength of the words; it is not merely that the sorrow would be changed *for* joy, but turned *into* joy; it is not merely the *exchange* of one thing for another, but the very cause of grief was itself to be turned into a matter of joy. Thus it has ever been, and thus it still is, with the true Zion of God. The tears which they shed are as good seed, which shall bring forth a harvest of joy; they are as water which it is the Lord's gracious purpose to turn into the wine of joy. 'Thou hast turned for me,' said David, 'my mourning into dancing' (Psa. 30:11). 'Blessed are they that mourn: for they shall be comforted' (Matt. 5:4).

But in order to show still more plainly the connection between true spiritual joy and godly sorrow, our Lord adds the following *simile*, taken from the prophet Isaiah (26:17–20), and which must have been sufficiently familiar to the minds of the disciples: 'A woman when she is in travail hath sorrow because her hour is come: but as soon as she is delivered of the child, she remembereth no more the anguish, for joy that a man is born into the world.' Who is here represented by the woman travailing in anguish? Clearly *the company of the disciples*—the church of God, which they represent. And what is the precise point of comparison between them? It is simply this—the great and sudden transition from the extremity of grief to the extremity of joy, and to this exclusively our attention ought to be directed. The expression 'her hour' alludes perhaps to the brevity of the anguish; it was to be but short—short as the hour of travail to a woman—while the word 'a man' brings out the greatness of the event, and the real cause of the mother's joy.

But *our Lord himself explains the comparison*: 'And ye now therefore have sorrow; but I will see you again, and your heart shall rejoice' (verse 22). What does our Lord refer to, when he says: 'I will see you again'? The meaning of these words is clearly determined by what follows. It is the great event of Pentecost, and not the resurrection, that is here spoken of. But you will carefully observe that there is here a certain change of the words from those which he had previously used. It is not now: 'A little while, and ye shall see me'; but it is: 'But I will see you again.' And what are we to make of these words? Brethren, the death of Jesus not only separated the disciples from him; but him also, in a sense, from them; he was no longer with them, as he was wont. So real was the separation on *both* sides. But when the Spirit comes, Christ comes; and after Pentecost, Jesus was among them in the presence and power of his Spirit in a richer, fuller sense than he had ever been before. It is just as if he said: 'I will return to visit you, to see you, and to bless you with showers of heavenly grace.'

And the *effect* of this visit our Lord describes in the following words: 'And your heart shall rejoice, and your joy no man taketh from you.' In the first place, their joy was to be a *heart* joy—a *great, deep, living* joy—when the Comforter would come; and then, secondly, *no man could take it from them*. It is true, indeed, that this life is a vale of tears; but it is also true that there is a joy in the Christian's heart of which the Spirit of God is the author, and of which no man—not even the devil, nor the world, nor the flesh—can ever deprive him.

Lastly here, our Lord points out the *inward, experimental secret* of this joy, viz., *fulness of spiritual knowledge and prayer in the name of Jesus*: 'And in that day ye shall ask me nothing,' or, rather, inquire of me nothing. 'Verily, verily, I say unto you, whatsoever ye shall ask the Father in my name, he will give it you' (verse 23). He refers to a definite day: 'And in that day.' The day of which Jesus speaks has already been more than once referred to. It is the long-promised, long-expected day of the Holy Spirit (Jer. 31:31-34). And this great joy of which he speaks is traced up to a two-fold blessing which the Holy Spirit was, from that day, to confer upon them. In the first place, there was to be *a fulness of knowledge.* 'Ye shall ask me nothing'; that is to say, they would ask him *no more questions*; they would not need to ask him to explain to them, as they were now doing, what might seem to them mysterious or obscure; for they would have 'the Spirit of truth,' to 'guide them into all truth.' And, moreover, there would now be conferred on them the spirit *of prayer in the name of Jesus.* 'Verily, verily I say unto you, whatsoever ye shall ask the Father in my name, he will do it' (verse 23). In this connection our Lord adds: 'Hitherto have ye asked nothing in my name,' his exaltation to the right hand of God being necessary to prayer in his name; yea, to this outpouring of the spirit of prayer. 'The Holy Spirit was not yet given, because Jesus was not yet glorified.' But he was now to be given after his departure. And therefore he adds: 'Ask, and ye shall receive'—ask when I am gone, and in my name—'and ye shall receive, that your *joy may be full.*' And thus would be fulfilled the promise given in verses 20 and 22. And thus, too, we see that the nearer we get to God in prayer, the nearer do we come to the goal of joy. Prayer is, as it were, the mighty steed that draws the chariot in which we ride to the gate of celestial joy. But we must not proceed further for the present. On a review of this whole passage, may we not observe:

In the first place, what *a wonderful teacher* is the Lord Jesus Christ! He makes statements and puts questions which are at first sight fitted to startle, to perplex, to puzzle his own. But they are only intended to excite enquiry, to draw forth questions from them to him; and then, when he has drawn forth their desires to the uttermost, he, who reads their hearts, proceeds to unravel the mystery. There are many things in God's dealings with his own that are very deep and mysterious; but they are all of the Lord's ordering, and sent in infinite wisdom and love. And however painful and perplexing they may be now, yet when they have wrought out the purposes of his grace, they shall be made plain in the end. 'What thou knowest not now, thou shalt know hereafter.'

And besides, do we not see here *the close connection which there is between godly sorrow and everlasting joy*: 'Your sorrow will be turned into joy.' And while in speaking of this way through sorrow to joy our Lord is immediately addressing himself to the troubled hearts of his disciples, he is also thinking of his whole future church, whose way in this world is through a vale of tears. There is a joy indeed, which shall end in eternal sorrow; but there is a sorrow, on the other hand—a godly sorrow on account of sin, and from love to the Saviour—which shall end in everlasting joy!

Finally, let us learn here that *all true spiritual joy is to be traced up to the divine Spirit as its author*. There is indeed a natural joy, and there are also sinful joys, which are as the crackling of thorns under a pot. But there is also a holy joy in God, every drop of which comes from above. Whence did all the joy promised to the disciples proceed? It came from the outpouring of the Spirit from on high. And how could they but rejoice, when they obtained the unction from on high?—when they got clearer views of the King in his beauty? How could they but rejoice, when their hearts were enlarged at the throne of grace? This is just what we all need still. May the Holy Spirit take of the things that are Christ's, and show them unto us!

Jesus Speaking Plainly of the Father—Last Farewell

John 16:25–33

THE connection between this passage and the preceding context is very clear and close. Jesus has been speaking of two great blessings that would accompany the gospel dispensation—the dispensation of the Spirit, viz., *fullness of knowledge* and *prayer in the name of Jesus*—liberty at the throne of grace (verse 23). And now in the opening verses of this passage, he takes up these two ideas again, and expands them more fully (25–27).

In the first instance, he takes up and develops the idea of *spiritual knowledge*. 'These things have I spoken unto you in proverbs'—in parables, in obscure, dark language, as opposed to the 'showing plainly' by the Spirit's teaching. Jesus had often, during the course of his ministry, made use of figurative or parabolic speech; he had done so repeatedly that very night—the Father's house, in which were many mansions; the vine and the branches; the woman in travail; his return to them; and

their seeing one another again—these are so many spec-
imens of his speaking in proverbs, or dark parables.
There is a sense indeed—an important sense—in which
all human language, all teaching by mere words, is but
a dark parable, only able to give us a *faint idea* of the
things of God, and not to express fully *the very things
themselves*. But then referring to the Spirit's teaching,
our Lord adds: 'But the time cometh, when I shall no
more speak unto you in parables, but I shall show you
plainly of the Father' (verse 25), that is clearly, powerfully, and *in a way commensurate with the truth itself*.
And mark you, Jesus says: 'I will show you plainly;' for
although the Spirit is the personal agent, yet when the
Spirit teaches, Jesus teaches; it is he that opens up the
way for the great teacher; it is he that sends the Comforter; it is of the things of Christ that the Spirit takes,
and shows them unto us: so that when the Spirit teaches,
Jesus teaches.

But our Lord takes up also and expands the other
idea, viz., that of *prayer in his name*: 'At that day ye
shall ask in my name'; and this of itself implies the
function of an intercessor. But he adds, 'And I say not
unto you, that I will pray the Father for you' (verse 26),
that is to say, he will not pray the Father for them, as
if the Father himself were not disposed to aid them.
Christ does indeed pray for his people; for already he
has said, 'I will pray the Father, and he shall give you
another Comforter' (14:16). Not a blessing comes from
the hand of a holy and just God, but comes through

the mediation and intercession of his Son. But, on the other hand, he does not pray the Father as if to incline an unwilling ear; or, as if for the purpose of extorting a blessing from unwilling hands. On the contrary, 'the Father himself loveth you,' and why? 'Because ye have loved me, and have believed that I came out from God' (verse 27). The order is, God first loved them, even when they were in their sins (Eph. 2:4–5); and it is because he did that they now love him; but now he loves again with a love of complacency, because they have loved Jesus, and have believed that he came out from God. Oh, how could it be otherwise? Yes, the Father loves those who have become one with him in love to the Son, and who believe that he sent him; and, therefore, while Jesus pleads with the Father for them, it is not as if to extort blessings from unwilling hands.

But now starting from this position—the position which they had admitted and believed, that he came out from God—our Lord proceeds to give *the true explanation of his going to the Father.* 'I came forth from the Father,' says he, 'and am come into the world; again, I leave the world and go to the Father' (verse 28). What the disciples could not comprehend at the first, what puzzled and perplexed, as well as grieved them, was that Jesus should depart out of this world, in which, as they supposed, he was to set up his kingdom. And besides this, they had but very confused ideas of the place to which he was going. In explaining to them the reason of his departure, Jesus sets out from what was more apparent to them to what was less so; they believed and admitted that he came forth from the Father—that behind and before his earthly existence in the flesh there was his pre-existence with the Father. If so, it plainly follows that this world was to him but a place of passage—a temporary abode—to which he came for a definite purpose, and to accomplish a definite work. What then more natural than that when this work was accomplished he should leave this world, and return to God from whom he came? Such I take to be the general scope and meaning of those very remarkable words (13:3).

Observe the *two-fold* movement of the Son of God; or, as the Apostle Paul elsewhere puts it, his descent and ascent (Eph. 4:9–10)—either movement having its *two-fold* aspect—the movement from heaven to earth in the words, 'I came forth from the Father, and am come into the world'; and the movement from earth to heaven in the words, 'Again, I leave the world, and go to the Father.' And notwithstanding the many attempts which have been made within recent years to reconstruct the old, or to formulate a new dogma, on the mysterious subject of the person and work of Christ—when these words are taken in connection with similar passages on the same subject (Phil. 2:6–7; 2 Cor. 8:9)—we believe that the old phrase of the *two natures in one person*, comes as near to the truth of God as the imperfections of human thought and language admit of. When Jesus says that he came forth from the Father, and was come into the world, what can these words mean, but that the eternal Son of God took human nature into such a mysterious union with his own divine person, that while now standing before them in human nature, he could say of *himself* that he came forth from the Father, and was come into the world? And when, again, he adds that he was now to leave the world and to go to the Father, what can his words mean, but that he was now, in the nature thus assumed, to ascend up on high, to be glorified with the glory which he had with the Father before the world was? while, at the same time, it is obvious that the former statement was meant to explain and vindicate the latter; in other words, the descent of Jesus explains the ascent; the humiliation the exaltation; the divine past of Jesus sheds a glorious light on the future.

And the truth is that the Saviour's words had *a powerful effect on their minds*, as appears from the following words: 'Lo, now speakest thou plainly, and speakest no parable' (verse 29). Not indeed that the promised time had come, when he would speak plainly of the Father. Still, however, there shone such a bright light around them in connection with the Saviour's words that they seemed to have nothing more to desire in respect of illumination; while, at the same time, by reading the thoughts which were secretly agitating their hearts, Jesus gave them a clear proof of his omniscience. That the words, 'Now we are sure that thou knowest all things, and needest not that any man should ask thee,' (verse 30), stand in closest relation to those of verse 19: 'Jesus knew that they were desirous to ask him,' no-one, we think, will be disposed to dispute. Like Nathanael, in the early days of our Lord's ministry, they had just experienced that he was omniscient—that he was the great searcher of hearts—and, therefore, like him, they inferred that he was divine. 'By this we believe,' say they, 'that thou camest forth from God' (verse 30).

And Jesus acknowledges this faith to be *real*: 'Jesus answered them, now ye believe' (verse 31). We must beware, indeed, of taking these words in an interrogative sense, as though Jesus had cast any doubt on the reality of their faith; for, in the intercessory prayer, he declares plainly, and in terms which certainly allude to this passage, 'They have known surely that I came out from thee, and they have believed that thou didst send me' (17:8). These words, then, are not to be taken as implying any doubt as to the reality of their faith, but rather as expressing a joyful affirmation. It is just as if he had said, 'Now ye have reached the point to which I have been labouring so long to conduct you. Now, at length, ye do believe.'

And yet the tie which bound them so close to him was soon to be subjected to a severe test: 'Behold the hour cometh; yea, is now come, that ye shall be scattered, every one of you to his own, and shall leave me alone' (verse 32). In using the word 'scattered,' the Lord refers to the passage in Zechariah 13:7, which tells of the shepherd being smitten, and the flock scattered, and which in Matthew 26:31 he applies directly to himself. Oh! surely it was another drop in the Saviour's cup of bitterness that he was thus left alone. That a deep and painful sense of injury sustained is here expressed, no one will deny. And yet, though they might leave him alone, there was one who would not utterly forsake him: 'And yet I am not alone, because the Father is with me.' And there is a sense in which the same thing is true of all his followers—no-one else having access to their hearts, there is an awful solitariness about their case; and yet the Father is with them in his special providence and sustaining grace. But, oh! who can tell how near the Father is to his own eternal Son? 'And yet I am not alone, because the Father is with me.'

And now our Lord *sums up this whole discourse by stating the great end he had in view in all these utterances*: 'These things have I spoken unto you'—not merely the preceding words, but this whole discourse, of which these are the last words. All that Jesus said to them during this last ever-memorable night was intended to inspire them with perfect peace in him. It is the peace of Shiloh, who, as the Lamb of God and the Lion of the tribe of Judah, has overcome (Gen. 49:10), and now rules for ever in his kingdom of peace. It is the peace of the heavenly Solomon, which the Shulamite extols as the crown of her heavenly felicity (Song of Sol. 3:11). It is the peace of 'the Prince of Peace' (Isa. 9:6-7), which he made by the shedding of his most precious blood. In this peace, which the Lord bequeaths to his disciples as *his* peace (14:27), is contained the whole fatness of the divine blessing, and it *lasts for ever.* This peace is to be enjoyed *in* Christ: 'That *in me* ye might have peace.' Oh, let us remember this—not only is he the author of it, having purchased it with his precious blood, but it is in him as the sphere within which it is to be enjoyed. And I may add, *it is the result of his own divine word*: 'These things have I spoken unto you,' for this very end, 'that in me ye might have peace.' His word brings peace, and this is what no power or might of man can effect for us. Oh, let us seek to say with David, 'Great peace have they who love thy law.' If only his word abide in us, there is buried within us the seed of peace, which the heavenly Comforter causes to spring up and bear fruit.

But the man who desires to have peace in Christ must accept also of the other part of the Christian's lot—tribulation in the world, for the world hates and persecutes the children of God. Observe the two opposite spheres—'in me,' 'in the world.' The one describes the sphere of peace; the other that of tribulation; in Christ, peace; in the world, tribulation. And if the world, in which there is tribulation, were merely *outside* of us, the case would not be so bad; but there are still *within* us remains of worldliness, and therefore we have tribulation often, which threatens to swallow up our peace. And yet, in the very presence of this tribulation, he exhorts them to 'be of good cheer.' Their peace was to assume the character of assurance and courage. And for a good reason: 'I have overcome the world'— not only *before* you, but *for* you; so that the same victory shall be accomplished in you as in me' (1 John 2:13; 5:4). Deep into the very heart of the Apostle John sank these blessed words of him who had overcome; and what is a great part of his first Epistle, and what is the entire book of the Revelation, but a repetition in capital letters of the words: 'They overcame by the blood of the Lamb, and by the word of his testimony'?

Let me now endeavour to sum up the *substance* of the teaching of this remarkable passage. We have seen here (1) *the unspeakable importance of the Spirit's work*. It is by the Spirit that Jesus speaks plainly of the Father; it is the Spirit alone that can speak to the heart in language commensurate with the truth. It is by the Spirit's grace that we learn to pray in the name of Jesus. (2) That while prayer is to be offered up in the name of Jesus; and while he is our intercessor with the Father— *it is not as if to extort blessings from unwilling hands*. On the contrary, the Father himself loves those for whom Jesus intercedes. Oh surely this intercession must prevail! The intercessor is the eternal Son of God—his well-beloved Son, his only begotten Son—who is in his bosom; and the Father himself also loves those for whom Jesus pleads. (3) That *the incarnation explains the ascension*. If the Son of God veiled his glory, and tabernacled in flesh, in order to accomplish a definite work, what more natural than that, when this work is finished, his battle fought, and his victory won, he should return to him from whom he came. (4) That *true faith must be tried*. The Lord has his fire in Sion, and his furnace in Jerusalem. The Lord sits as the refiner of the gold. Oh what need to pray that we may be preserved in the day of trial! But finally (5) we see here that there is peace only in Jesus—in living union and fellowship with him—but *in him there is solid, substantial, everlasting peace*. What though there be tribulation in the world, their covenant Head has overcome the world; and through his blood and by his grace, they also shall be victorious.

III

THE INTERCESSORY PRAYER

John 17

'Father, Glorify Thy Son'
John 17:1–5

J ESUS has already manifested his love to 'his own' in wonderful ways indeed. He has *acted* and he has *spoken*. He has performed that remarkable act of washing the disciples' feet, so full of divine condescension and so symbolical of spiritual truth; and he has uttered those glorious sayings, so full of heavenly light and love. And yet he is not done; to these inestimable proofs of his love he will add yet another jewel in this sublime intercessory prayer, in which he seems to gather up as into one focus all the light and glory of the preceding chapters.

This prayer has usually been divided into three great parts: First of all, Jesus prays for *himself*—for his being glorified (verses 1–5); then, secondly, for the apostles that were then before him, the first ordained preachers of the word (verses 6–19); and, thirdly, for the entire body of believers, in all places and at all times, to the end of the world (verses 20–24). Thus does Jesus pray first for himself, next for the apostles, and lastly, for the catholic church of God. It is not, however, as if there were no very close relation between the several parts; on the contrary, there is a golden principle which underlies and unites them all. For when Jesus prays for himself, that he may be glorified, it is that he may also glorify the Father by giving eternal life to as many as he had given him (verses 1, 2); when he prays for the apostles, it is that they—being themselves, in the first instance, partakers of it—might be the honoured instruments and agents in his hand in perpetuating and extending the knowledge of that salvation to the ends of the earth; and when again he commends to God all believers— future as well as present—it is because they were to be *the objects* on whom eternal life was to be conferred— the sphere within which the glory of God was to be displayed in the salvation of their souls. So that, while the general branches of the prayer are indeed such as I have indicated, the one great principle which unites and pervades them all is *the glory of God in the salvation of men*. It is in short a prayer for the manifestation of the divine glory in the communication of eternal life unto his people.

And moreover, it may further be premised here that Jesus *spoke aloud* the emotions which now filled his heart. He not only prayed, but he prayed audibly; which plainly intimates that while he was speaking to God, he was also speaking for the benefit of those around him. This I take to be fairly implied in the words: 'And these things I speak in the world'—speak aloud in the world; for this is the real meaning of the word. It was no *secret* meditation, therefore, but *audible* speech. It is just as if he had said: 'It is in heaven that I am to be carrying on my intercessory work for ever, but these things I speak audibly in the world, and this, too, that they might have my joy fulfilled in themselves.' That is to say, Jesus had ineffable joy in offering up this prayer, in the fellowship which he had with the Father, and in the assurance which he possessed of being heard in their behalf; and he desires that they should become sharers with him in that joy. And oh! what must have been the feelings of the disciples as they listened to this prayer! How the face of Jesus must have shone forth as the sun, and his words sounded as the very music of heaven, as this prayer ascended up on high!

But I must still further observe, by way of preliminary, that this has been called Christ's *priestly prayer*. It is, indeed, the act of the great High Priest of the church, offering up to God himself and all his people, both present and future; while, at the same time, it is obvious that this prayer brings down upon them the blessing of God. For what Jesus here asks, Jesus *obtains*. Yes, brethren, this prayer was answered, is being answered still, and will continue to be answered, until the last vessel of mercy is gathered home to glory (verse 24). What a rich and precious portion, therefore, of the word of God have we here! No wonder that the church, for whom the head and High Priest offered up this prayer of eternal power and efficacy, has ever regarded it as one of her most precious treasures; and that she has been accustomed to refresh herself from it, as from a stream of living water, the most abundant. No wonder, though many men of God have said: 'This chapter is the simplest in all the Bible in words, but the most profound in meaning.' And what need, therefore, have you and I of the Spirit's teaching as we now proceed to open up its several parts in their order!

First then—and for the present—let us hear Jesus praying for himself—for his being glorified (verses 1–5). Thus does the inspired Evangelist introduce the subject: 'These words,' that is, the whole of the preceding discourse, 'spake Jesus and lifted up his eyes to heaven.' It is but very seldom that the apostle describes the gestures or looks of our blessed Lord. But this appears to have been an occasion on which the impression was indelible, and therefore the upward look must not be passed over. How much more natural, too, and significant does this action become, on the supposition that it was performed out of doors, than if we adhere to the idea that they were still in the upper room (14:31; Mark 14:26). As he raised his eyes to heaven, Jesus said: 'Father'—not *our* Father, as though putting himself on the same level with them; for although indeed God is their Father in Christ, yet, after all, there is an infinite difference in this respect, between him and them—between the sense in which he is their Father by regenerating and adopting grace—and the sense in which he is the Father of him 'who is the brightness of his glory, and the express image of his person.' Nor yet does he say: '*My* Father,' as in Gethsemane, which would put too great a separation between him and them for such a prayer as this—but simply 'Father,' as bringing out the divine relation between the Father and the Son. And if you glance your eye along the chapter, you will find that *six* different times does Jesus use the title Father in this prayer—four times without any qualifying adjective, and twice with a distinguishing epithet as 'holy Father,' and 'righteous Father' (verses 1, 5, 11, 21, 24, 25). And it may be truly said that the whole spirit of the prayer which follows is concentrated in this title of Father. The whole tone that distinguishes it, from first to last, is that of filial love and confidence. Addressing him as Father, he says: 'The hour is come.' What hour? The hour of his death—the hour stipulated in the everlasting covenant between the Father and the Son—the hour of which Jesus often said to the Jews: 'Mine hour is not yet come'—the hour on which were suspended the glory of his Father and the eternal destiny of myriads—that hour had now at last struck. And what more, therefore, does he now say? 'Father, glorify thy Son, that thy Son also may glorify thee.'

[1] What, then, in the first place, is the *import* of this prayer? What is he really praying for when he says, 'glorify thy Son'? I know indeed, that many interpreters, understanding by this glorifying the *moral perfections and beauties* which Jesus was to manifest in his

sufferings, give to this prayer the meaning: '*Countenance me, sustain me, strengthen me in this hour of trial!*' And there can be no question that the Father, by his Spirit, did sustain his holy humanity: 'Behold my servant whom I uphold—I will put my Spirit upon him.' But this explanation is not consistent with verse 5, which dearly proves that Jesus is thinking of his restoration to that glory which he had with the Father before the world was. Others again understand this prayer as referring to the attractive power which Jesus would henceforth exercise upon the minds of men, and by means of which he would be glorified in their hearts. But this view is equally opposed to verse 5, from which it appears that Jesus is evidently speaking, not of what he is to be in the view and experience of others, but of restoration to glory in *his own person*. What Jesus is here asking is that through his death now just at hand, and as the reward of his finished work, he might be exalted to the right hand of God, that there—in this new position—he also might glorify the Father, by applying the redemption which he had wrought out upon the earth.

And you observe that he speaks of himself *objectively*, in the third person. He does not say, glorify me, but 'glorify thy Son'—as if he designedly meant to bring out the relation in which he stood to the Father. It is as the Son that he now addresses the Father, and it is as the Son that he now asks to be glorified. Who does not see in this the proof of conscious equality with the Father? Where is the mere creature that could go before his maker and say, 'Glorify thy Son, that thy Son also may glorify thee'? And yet Jesus could say it: 'Glorify thy Son, that thy Son also, in his turn, may glorify thee.'

[2] And the view which we have now given you harmonises exactly with the explanatory statement, which immediately follows: 'As thou hast given him power over all flesh, that whatsoever thou hast given him, to them he should give eternal life' (verse 2). In the opening words of this remarkable sentence, Jesus shows that what he had now been praying for was in accordance with a decree which had already been passed: 'Glorify thy Son that thy Son also may glorify thee, even as'—in a manner corresponding to what follows—intimating to us plainly that in praying thus he was only asking what was in harmony with the decree of God himself. But our Lord next states *the purpose* for which the Father had given him this power or authority over all flesh. 'That whatsoever thou hast given him, to them he should give eternal life.' Observe *the three-fold gift* of which Jesus here speaks. The Father has given the Son authority—absolute authority—over all flesh. But he has also given him a people to be saved. And now the Saviour declares that *the purpose* for which the Father has given him this absolute and universal power is that whatsoever the Father gave him, to them he might give eternal life.

But it deserves to be specially noticed that as these two verses are in exact accord, it plainly follows from the very structure of the sentence that the purpose expressed in verse 1, 'That thy Son also may glorify thee', corresponds precisely to that expressed in verse 2: 'That he should give eternal life to as many as thou hast given him.' So that when we take into account the close connection between the two statements it just comes to this, that the Son was to glorify the Father by communicating eternal life to as many as the Father had given him. Blessed combination—the glory of the Father and the eternal life of his people! Let us rejoice to know that in the cross of Christ these two are gloriously harmonised. By presenting the aim of his prayer under this new aspect of it, he was also urging it on new grounds. It is just as if he had said: Glorify thy Son that thy Son also may glorify thee, by giving, in conformity with the mandate which thou hast given him, eternal life to as many as thou hast given him.

And who does not see here the *security—the absolute certainty of the final salvation*—of all God's chosen people? If the Father has given to the Son absolute and universal power for this very purpose, that he should bestow on them eternal life, how can they possibly come short of it? Nay, it is impossible; though earth and hell should combine against the Lord and his anointed, Jehovah's purpose shall be accomplished. All attempts to thwart it are weaker than a cobweb before the loaded cannon's mouth. In a word, he gave him 'to be the head over all things to the church, which is his body, the fulness of him that filleth all in all' (Eph. 1:22–23).

[3] But having once mentioned the great blessing of eternal life, our Lord next proceeds to trace *the very close and profound connection which there is between the bestowal of this gift and glorifying the Father*. For this purpose he pauses to contemplate the nature of eternal life; he describes its real, essential character; and this is the definition which he gives of it: 'And this is life eternal, that they might know thee, the only true God, and Jesus Christ whom thou hast sent' (verse 3).

Observe, it is not said merely this is the way to eternal life, but this is life eternal *itself*—'to know thee.' Eternal life, then, is not mere conscious and unending existence, but it is 'to know thee.' It is not, however, *any* or *every* kind of knowledge of which Jesus here speaks; it is not mere head or rational knowledge—the mere natural information of the mind, or the excitation of the feelings; but it is that living, personal, and experimental knowledge—that knowledge, which includes oneness in will with God, and partaking of his nature; it is the knowledge, love, and enjoyment of him who is infinite; it is that knowledge which is the result of the work of the Spirit glorifying Jesus and with him God in us.

And oh, how glorious *the object* of this knowledge! To know *thee*, but thee, the *only true God*. It is impossible not to see in the word '*only*' the opposition to the many gods, unworthy of the name, of the heathen nations around. But this is 'the *only true* God,' that is, the only being that perfectly answers to the idea involved in the word 'God.' There might be, and there were, gods many, but this is the only God that meets all that is involved in the name—the only true God, in contrast to all the idols of the heathen, and to all the gods that are still worshipped amongst men.

But *how* am I to get at the true and saving knowledge of this God? It is only in Jesus Christ whom he has sent. 'I am the way,' says Jesus, 'the truth, and the life;' 'He that hath seen me hath seen the Father.' It is a remarkable fact that this is the only place where our Lord gives himself this compound title of Jesus Christ, afterwards so common in apostolic preaching and writing. And most destructive is the use which infidel and rationalistic writers have attempted to make of this fact, as if it proved the fictitious character of this prayer; or, in other words, that it is a composition of a later date than the time of our Lord. But the answer to this infidel objection is not far to seek. There were many reasons, of the strongest character, why Jesus should refrain from giving himself the title of Christ before the common people, subject as that title was to so much misconception. He did not desire to precipitate the awful crisis of his final sufferings; and therefore he ordinarily spoke of himself under the title of the Son of man. But the time had now arrived when the full name of gospel peace—the glorious title made up of the two words 'Jesus Christ'—was to be proclaimed to the ends of the earth. Was it not, therefore, highly necessary that the disciples should, for once at least, hear it from the

Master's own blessed lips? Could they afterwards have made such use of this symbol of the Christian faith, if he had continued to the very last in keeping apart the two most significant names of which it is composed? And under what more advantageous circumstances, in what more worthy or solemn form, could Jesus have uttered it than now, in their own hearing, and in this last act of communion with his Father?

And who does not see here also another evidence, by implication, of the eternal Godhead of Jesus? The juxtaposition in which he is here placed with the Father as the object of that knowledge, which is not only the source, but the very essence of eternal life, is to us the dearest evidence that this is the true God and eternal life.

Now if this is eternal life—if it consists in the saving knowledge, love, enjoyment, and service of God—then it plainly follows that the most effectual means of glorifying God is to communicate this life to the souls of men.

[4] But now, after this description of the life which he was to bestow, Jesus returns to the prayer of verse 1. He mentions what he had already done to glorify the Father (verse 4), and then he reiterates his request for restoration to his divine glory (verse 5).

In the first instance, he mentions what he had already done to glorify the Father: 'I have glorified thee on the earth,' etc.; or rather, 'I glorified thee,' in the past tense, for the thing is conceived as past and finished. It is most important to preserve in the translation the past tense used in the original; otherwise it might be supposed that the work referred to was only what he had done before uttering this prayer, whereas our Lord really included in this finished work all that he had done on earth including the decease which he should afterwards accomplish at Jerusalem. It is just as if our Lord said: 'I have done all that can be done to glorify thee in my earthly state; thou gavest me a work to do; I finished it, I gave it the last stroke. And now'—in return—'glorify thou me.' And here the words—'I thee,' and 'thou me'— are so placed each beside its fellow, as to show that it is a perfect reciprocity of service that our Lord means to express. 'I thee glorified,' and now in return, 'thou me glorify.'

But oh, what a prayer! 'Glorify thou me, with thine own self.' And if you ask what this means, I can only say it is explained in the words which follow: 'With the glory which I had with thee before the world was.' Christ had a glory with the Father before the world was, even from all eternity; that glory was veiled or eclipsed when he tabernacled upon earth; with this glory he now seeks to be reinvested—not, however, simply as before, but now in our nature. And this prayer has been answered; what Jesus here asks, Jesus has obtained. Christ *is* now glorified in our nature at God's right hand.

And now in bringing these remarks to a close for the present, observe *the two-fold end* which Christ had in view in offering up this prayer—the glory of the Father and the salvation of his people. What do we make the great end of our being? Do we resemble the blessed Master in this? O, let us remember that we can never glorify God except by becoming partakers of that life which consists in the knowledge, love, and enjoyment of God.

And notice also *the ground* on which Jesus prayed for his being glorified—his finished work—the cross. The cross is the foundation of all the glory that now encircles him as Mediator. And if it was on this ground that he prayed to be reinvested with his glory, oh! let us rest assured of it that it is only through the cross that ever we can reach the crown. The Lord enable us to say: 'God forbid that I should glory save in the cross of our Lord Jesus Christ.'

Christ Praying for the Apostles—
Preservation

John 17:6–19

IN the preceding section our Lord prays for himself—
for his being glorified—and this, too, that in this new
position at the right hand of God he might glorify the
Father by communicating eternal life to those that he
had given him. But he will not accomplish this object
except through instruments and agents, whom he has
raised up and prepared for the purpose. Accordingly,
prayer for himself as the *author* of our salvation is naturally followed up by prayer for the apostles, as the
honoured instruments in his hand, for perpetuating and
transmitting the knowledge of that salvation to the ends
of the earth.

Here, then, we have, in the first place, a *preface* or
introduction, which prepares the way (verses 6–8);
then, secondly, comes *the prayer itself*, which is at first
of a more general character (verses 9, 10), but which
afterwards branches out into two definite and distinct
petitions: 'keep them' (verses 11–15), 'sanctify them'

(17–19). Let us consider this prayer somewhat more particularly as thus briefly sketched.

[1] With reference to the first of these—the introduction or preface—Jesus says: 'I have manifested thy name unto the men whom thou gavest me out of the world,' etc. I may premise in general that the great prevailing idea expressed in these first three verses (6–8) is the *preciousness* of these souls—the unspeakable value which they have acquired in consequence of the ministry of Jesus.

1. Notice, therefore, in the first instance, *what Jesus himself did for them*: 'I have manifested thy name'—thy character—thy name as the eternal Father—'unto them.' And how did he do it? By revealing himself to them and in them as the eternal Son. 'He that hath seen me hath seen the Father' (14:9). He who with the eye of faith has seen Jesus Christ knows also God's most wonderful revelation—his all-holy name. From the manger at Bethlehem to the grave of Joseph of Arimathea, from Jordan to the brook Cedron, from the mount of transfiguration to the hill of Golgotha, the whole of Christ's life, his sufferings and death, ay, and afterwards his resurrection—is nothing but the most lucid and blessed revelation of the name of God, by which he would be known of us. Yes, brethren, Jesus reveals the Father by revealing himself; and this is the reason that his testimony concerning himself was, as we see from this fourth Gospel, an essential element of his teaching.

2. But having mentioned what he had done for them and in them, Jesus proceeds to state *what the Father himself had done for them*: 'The men,' says he, 'whom thou gavest me out of the world.' They were once of the world—not only *in* it, as their habitation, but *of* it—of its spirit and disposition—of the world that lies in the wicked one—but thou hast chosen them out of it, and given them to me in a day of thy grace and power. 'Thine they were'—not merely as men, and as Jews, but as objects of thine everlasting love. 'And thou gavest them me'—not only in thine eternal purpose, but by the inward effectual drawing of the Spirit, so often spoken of in this Gospel: 'All that the Father giveth me shall come to me' (6:37). 'Every one that hath heard and hath learned of the Father cometh to the Son' (6:45).

3. But now, thirdly, Jesus passes on to *what the apostles themselves had done*. They had kept intact and entire the word, which had been committed to them. Jesus says: 'They have kept thy word'—*thy* word, *not* mine. For his word was only a faithful reproduction of the Father's; and the disciples had been able, through his divine manifestation, to discern this profound relation, and to recognise in the teaching which Jesus had given to them that which the Father had given to him. Is not this the meaning of the following words: 'Now they have known that all things whatsoever thou hast given me are of thee'? The Father had given all these things to the Son; and now they were enabled to perceive that these things were of the Father. For, in point

of fact, Jesus had given the very words of his Father (verse 8). 'And they have received them'; that is, in simple faith, on the authority of the divine testimony; 'and have known surely that I came out from thee'—referring to *his divine relation to the Father*, as pointed out in 16:28—'and they have believed that thou didst send me'—referring to *his divine mission*.

Thus does Jesus introduce the objects of his love to the Father. He states what he had done for them; what the Father himself had done for them; and what they themselves, in consequence of his revealing the Father to them, were enabled to do. 'These,' he would say, 'are the men whose case I desire to plead.'

[2] And now, secondly, having prepared the way for the prayer, Jesus states it; having introduced the objects of his love, by telling all about them, he now begins to plead in their behalf: 'I pray for them' (verse 9); or, rather, 'I for them pray.' The 'I' stands out prominently first—I, thine eternal Son—I who have laboured to bring them up to this point. And then immediately after, and before the word 'pray,' follow the words, which express the objects of his care: 'I for them'—those precious jewels—the result of all my labours, and so dear to thee and to me—'I for them now intercede.'

But just as if to bring out the objects of this intercession still more dearly and emphatically, they are described both negatively and positively—negatively in the words: 'I pray not for the world;' or, rather, 'not for the world I pray;' and positively in the words: 'But for them whom thou hast given me.' But most assuredly, when Jesus says, 'Not for the world I pray,' this is not to be understood *absolutely*, as if meaning that in no sense *whatever* did he pray for any that were still of the world. On the contrary, there were thousands of the world at that moment who were the objects of his everlasting love, and who were afterwards to be brought in. Witness, for example, what is said in verse 20 of this very chapter: 'Neither pray I for these alone, but for them also who shall believe on me through their word.' And certainly Jesus never meant to say that in no sense whatever did he pray for these. On the contrary, did he not say on the cross: 'Father, forgive them, for they know not what they do'? And that prayer was answered on the day of Pentecost. It is clear, then—clear as a sunbeam—that these words are not to be understood in an *absolute* sense, as meaning that in no sense whatever did he pray for any that were still of the world. But, on the other hand, we are to understand our Lord as meaning that he did not offer up *this* prayer for the world. No, but for those whom the Father had given him.

And who were these? Let the following passages from the context answer the question: 'I have manifested thy name unto the men whom thou gavest me'; 'They have kept thy word'; 'They have known that I came out from thee, and have believed that thou didst send me'; and again, 'I am glorified in them.' From all these passages it is clear that Jesus is speaking of *believers* as distinct from unbelievers. And the same thing is equally clear from *the nature of the blessings sought*. What the world needs is *converting grace*—grace to translate from darkness to God's marvellous light; but what Jesus here asks is that they may be kept (verse 11), and sanctified (verse 17)—blessings suited only to those who are already in a state of grace. On the whole, then, it is perfectly manifest that our Lord is here pleading for believers as distinct from unbelievers, for those that were already in a state of grace as distinct from those that were still in a state of nature; in short, for the eleven disciples that were now before him; and for these, too, as representatives, in a manner, of all believers to the end of the world.

And if you carefully look at the passage, you will find, that Jesus uses a *two-fold argument* in pleading in their behalf. (1) In the first instance, he pleads the relation in which they stood both to him and the Father—the mutual interest that they had in them: 'Thine', says he, 'whom thou hast given me.' 'Father, they are not strangers to thee, for whom I pray, but the very same whom thou hast given me, not only in the counsels of peace, but also in a day of grace and power. Father, it is thine own gift to me for whom I plead.' And all the more precious must they be to the Father, since in giving them to Christ, they did not cease to be his own: 'For they are thine,' says Jesus. Observe here the change from the past to the present tense. In verse 6 Jesus says: 'Thine they *were*'; but here it is: 'Thine they *are*', to convey the idea, that they are still the Father's. 'They were thine before thou gavest them to me, and they are thine still, only by closer and nearer ties.' And he adds: 'all mine are thine.' 'Oh, but anybody can say that; for all that we have belongs to God.' But look at the other side of it: 'And thine are mine.' None but the eternal Son of God could say this. And whereas the English version may give you the impression that persons only are meant, the truth is that *all things*, in the widest sense, are here claimed. 'Thy perfections, thy counsels, thy works, yea, the Godhead itself, are mine.'

(2) But, secondly, he pleads *the fact that they have become the depositories of his glory*: 'And I am glorified in them' (verse 10)—not only *by* them but *in* them—in their very state and character. Notwithstanding the lowly state of a servant in which he appeared, Jesus had revealed himself to their hearts in all his beauty as the Son of God; so that he was recognised by them for what he truly was, before he was restored to his original glory. And if in this, so also in other respects, he was glorified in them. He was glorified in their life of faith and holiness; in their obedience and sufferings. And it is just as if he had said: 'Father, my declarative glory in the world is connected with these. What is to become of my glory in the world, if any of these should perish?'

But from this point the prayer branches out into two distinct and definite petitions—'Keep them' (verse 11), and 'sanctify them' (verse 17).

1. With reference to the first of these petitions, *the occasion*, yea *the necessity*, of it is thus briefly stated: 'And now I am no more in the world.' Jesus speaks of himself as though he were already beyond this earthly scene. But although he speaks of himself as if he were no more in the world, yet they were in it: 'But these are in the world.' 'Though my struggles are now at an end, yet theirs are not.' And he adds: 'And I come to thee.' Oh! there is something deeply affecting in this reiterated reference to his own departure. It would seem as if his heart were overflowing with the most tender concern for those that were to be left struggling behind.

And what, therefore, next? 'Holy Father, keep through', or rather *in*, 'thine own name those whom thou hast given me'—keep those vessels of mercy, so precious to thee and to me, but henceforth to be exposed to so much danger. And this title, 'Holy Father,' how appropriate to the petition presented! This is, perhaps, the only instance in which the title is used by him. The attribute stands opposed to the evil that is in the world; and by the use of it, Jesus appeals to that perfection of the Father's nature, to keep them from being contaminated by the unholy atmosphere of the world, in which they were to be left behind; while the words, 'In thy name,' make the revelation of the divine character which was granted them, the enclosing wall, as it were, within which they were to be kept.

But our Lord refers, in the following verse, to *the faithfulness and diligence, with which he had kept them while he was with them*: 'While I was with them in the world, I kept them in thy name,' etc. (verse 12). Jesus here compares his keeping of them to that of the Father, in such a way as is accountable only on the supposition of both persons being of equal power and authority. Yea, he *watched over* them—as the second word here rendered *keep* properly signifies. And so *successfully* did he watch over them that none of them was lost, but the son of perdition, that the Scripture might be fulfilled. Are we, then, to infer from this that Judas was reckoned by Jesus in the number of those whom the Father had given him? No, certainly not (John 6:70-71). Judas was lost not as one given by the Father to the Son, but in order that the Scriptures might be fulfilled. The remark is simply parenthetical, and intended to justify the Lord's perfect watchfulness and care, *notwithstanding* the loss of Judas.

But our Lord returns once more to the subject of his own departure, and he declares that these things he spake in the world—spake *aloud*, for this is the real meaning of the word—that they might have his joy fulfilled in themselves (verse 13). He desires to initiate them into the very joy with which he himself is now filled. But the question may be raised, What is this joy? Is it the joy which he experienced in the expectation of his own speedy return to the Father? Or, is it the joy caused by the assurance that the Father would take them under his protecting care? Both these elements of joy mingled in his heart, and ought also to mingle in theirs. But most undoubtedly the context leads us to believe that it is the latter of which Jesus here speaks. In other words, Jesus is filled with joy in the sure anticipation that the Father himself would take them under his preserving care; and he speaks these things audibly in the world that they may share with him in his joy.

But without pursuing this subject further for the present, let us learn here, first *the character of God's true people*, who have an interest in this intercession. For while he has in view certainly the peculiar position and circumstances of the apostles, yet he regards them as representatives of all who might be similarly situated to the end of the world. And most precious are the evidences here given by which they may be known. 'I have manifested thy name unto the men whom thou gavest me.' 'They have received' and 'kept thy word'; 'they have known that I came out from thee, and that thou didst send me.' Are not these blessed marks of a work of grace?—the inward revelation of the divine glory; the receiving and the keeping of his blessed word; and faith in his divine origin and mission.

But, second, see *the dangers by which God's people are beset in the wilderness*. For certainly, when Jesus prays—keep them—it is implied that there are dangers from within and without—dangers from an evil heart of unbelief, from an evil world, and from the wicked one, who goes about like a roaring lion seeking whom he may devour. But if such is the danger, how suitable the prayer: 'Keep them.' Do it thyself! They cannot keep themselves, but thou canst keep them; 'let thine ever-lasting arms be around them and underneath them.' And there is not a child of God now on earth but is indebted to Jesus for this prayer.

Lastly, how blessed to know that *there is a friend in court—an intercessor within the veil*! For what is Jesus now doing at the right hand of God? Pleading with a continuous, ceaseless, special intercession for his own. Does sin plead loud against you? The blood of Jesus pleads louder still. Does Satan stand at your right hand to accuse you? Your advocate stands at God's right hand to plead for you. And Jesus is an advocate that never lost, and never will lose, any case committed to his care: 'If any man sin, we have an advocate with the Father, Jesus Christ the righteous.'

Christ Praying for the Apostles—Preservation—Consecration

John 17:14–19

THIS section, from verse 6 to verse 19, contains our Lord's prayer for the apostles; and a most wonderful prayer it is. He begins by stating what he had done for them, what the Father himself had done for them, and also what they, by the grace of God, had been able to do. And then, having thus shown their unspeakable *preciousness*, he proceeds to plead for them: 'I for them pray.' After noticing, in our last exercise, *the objects* of this prayer, or the persons that he prays for, namely, believers as distinct from the unbelieving world; and also *the grounds* on which he pleads—namely, the *relation* in which they stood to him and the Father, and the *fact* that he was glorified in them—we took up the first of the two *special* petitions: 'Holy Father, keep in thine own name those whom thou hast given me.'

But in the words with which we commence our present meditation, their need of divine preservation is still more particularly and urgently set forth: 'I have given them thy word, and the world hath hated them, because they are not of the world, as I am not of the world' (verse 14). Notice (1) what Jesus did: 'I have given them thy word'; (2) what the world did: 'And the world hath hated them'; and notice (3) the cause of the world's hatred: 'Because they are not of the world, as I am not of the world'. Or, in other words, the Father's word, which Jesus had given them, had detached them from the world, had made them in a manner as really strangers to it, as was Jesus himself; and therefore, like him, they had become the objects of the world's hatred (15:18–21).

And what then? Shall he at once take them home to be for ever with himself? Shall he transplant them at once into the paradise above? Shall he gather his wheat at once into his garner? Nay, but he will still leave them for a time in the world, to be a blessing by their testimony: 'I pray not that thou shouldest take them out of the world' (verse 15). Indeed, it was for the very purpose of preparing them for a mission to the world that he had separated them from it (verses 17, 18); and therefore, he will leave them for a time in it, after his own departure. They were to be the lights of the world, and the salt of the earth (Matt. 5:13–14). And oh! how much of the mercy of God to sinners is thus to be seen in his leaving the objects of his love in this sinful, persecuting world, that they may bless it with their life and testimony. It is true indeed, the world does not think so; right gladly would it get rid of God's witnesses. Nevertheless the fact remains that it is for their sakes that the world is permitted to stand. The old world could not be destroyed with the deluge, until Noah is safe in the ark. Sodom and Gomorrah and the cities of the plain could not be destroyed with fire and brimstone, until Lot is placed beyond all danger. But woe to the old world when once God has shut Noah into the ark! woe to the cities of the plain when once Lot has reached Zoar! And in like manner, woe to an ungodly world, when God has taken 'his own' home! It will then be fit only for the burning. Yes, it is an unspeakable mercy to the world that the Lord leaves the objects of his love for a time in it.

But while he was thus willing to leave them for a time here, still, however, the line of demarcation between them and the world was not to be obliterated. No, but whilst remaining in it, they were to be kept free from its contaminating influences. Hence Jesus closes this part of the prayer by reiterating the petition of verse 15 in a still more definite form: 'But that thou shouldest keep them from the evil.' 'I pray not that thou shouldest take them out of the world as a locality, but that thou shouldest keep them from the evil,' that is, all evil *in* and *of* the world. And certainly, as already hinted, when Jesus thus prays that they may be kept from the evil, it plainly implies the terrible character of the danger, to which his people are exposed in the world—a danger so great that it needs the constant interposition of divine grace to preserve them from it. Oh how blessed to know that Jesus still, from the throne of his glory, sees all the dangers to which his people are exposed; that he regards them still with the same tender care; and that him the Father hears always!

But from the prayer, 'Keep them,' which is rather negative, and which refers to their own salvation, Jesus passes on to the second petition, 'Sanctify' (verse 17), or rather, 'consecrate them;' which is more of a positive character, and which refers to their mission into the world. To prepare the way for this request, he reiterates the words, 'They are not of the world, even as I am not of the world' (verse 16). If they were not of the world, even as he was not of the world, although they were left for a time in it—hence their need of divine consecration, in order to the fulfilment of their mission. The word which is here rendered 'sanctify' properly signifies to *set apart*, to *consecrate* to a religious use. It is by no means synonymous with another word usually rendered to purify, to cleanse. Whenever any person or thing was set apart, under the Old Testament, to the service of God, that person or thing was said to be sanctified or consecrated (Exod. 29:1–36; 40:13; Lev. 22:2–3; Matt. 23:17). And just in express allusion to this, Jesus here prays that they may be set apart or consecrated to the service of God. It is true indeed that, as a matter of *fact*, the Lord does cleanse his people from the moral defilement of sin; but the sole idea conveyed to us by this word is that of separation or consecration to a religious use. That this is the exact meaning of the word is sufficiently obvious from the fact that the same word is applied in verse 19 to the Lord Jesus himself. In asking, then, that he would consecrate them, Jesus desires that their whole talents, strength, and life, should be devoted to this great work of the salvation of souls. This is a high idea of Christian holiness; and here it is viewed as about to be realised, specially under the form of the Christian ministry.

And besides, *the means* of consecration are specially pointed out: 'Through thy truth'—God's revealed truth as the medium—a statement of the highest practical importance (15:3; Col. 1:5; Eph. 1:13). I know indeed that some translate: 'in the truth,' as if it meant only the *element* of truth, in which he had placed them. But then, in that case, why should Jesus have added, 'Thy word is truth'? Is it not the end and aim of these words, to represent the word of God as the means by which the consecration was to be effected? And most undoubtedly the word of which Jesus speaks is the word which he had received from the Father, and which he in his instructions had delivered unto them (verses 8 and 14).

But our Lord now adduces *two great arguments*, or *reasons*, why he should obtain what he is now asking for them—the one taken from *the mission which he had conferred on them*, and the other from *the great work which he had himself, in his own person, done on their behalf*.

In the first place, Jesus pleads as a reason for their consecration *the mission on which he had sent them*: 'As thou hast sent me into the world, even so have I also

sent them into the world' (verse 18). If Jesus had asked
for them the Spirit of their office, it was because he had
already committed to them that great trust. And just as
the Father had sent him into the world, so, in another
sense, he had sent them into the world. But how does he
speak of sending them into the world, when they were
already in it? Because though they were in it, they were
not *of* it; he had raised them to a sphere above the world
(verse 14); and therefore he speaks of sending them into
it as into a foreign country. And if he sends them thither,
it is that they, as his commissioned servants, as his
instruments, may continue to carry on the work which
was commenced by himself. This, then, is the first reason
which he assigns for the petition, 'Consecrate them.' The
great work to which they have been called, and on which
they are sent forth, absolutely requires this.

But the second reason, stated in verse 19 is: 'And for
their sakes, I sanctify myself that they also might be
sanctified through the truth.' It is a beautiful, as well as a
most significant fact, that Jesus never asks anything from
the Father for them, without having done everything that
depended on himself for the fulfilment of his request.
Does he ask that they may be kept (verses 11 and 15).
Then he says: 'While I was with them in the world, I kept
them in thy name' (verse 12). And does he pray here:
'Consecrate them through thy truth'? Then he adds: 'And
for their sakes I sanctify myself'. It is just as if he had
said: 'And in order to obtain this consecration for them,
I begin by consecrating myself in their room and stead.'

The word 'sanctify' here, as we have already seen, by no means implies the removal of moral defilement or impurity; for it is not synonymous with purify or cleanse. Hence those interpreters are fearfully at fault, who find in this expression, as they imagine, a proof of original sin in Christ. Far from us be the blasphemous thought! On the contrary, we know that his human nature was 'holy, harmless, undefiled, and separate from sinners;' that he 'knew no sin.' The expression means neither more nor less than consecration to a holy use; and in the present connection and circumstances, it can only mean *his voluntary consecration of himself by offering himself up a sacrifice in their room and stead.* And there are just two glorious truths, as it appears to us, that are here suggested or revealed to us.

(1) The first truth suggested by these words is that of *the Redeemer's person and works*, or, in other words, that *Christ is both priest and sacrifice.* For mark you what it is that Jesus consecrates. Not all the cattle upon a thousand hills; not thousands of rivers of oil, but *himself.* Other priests offered up other sacrifices; but Jesus offered up *himself.* But how could this be? Was it not in the human nature only that he obeyed and suffered? Assuredly it was; but the human nature of Christ never existed separately and by itself, but, from the very moment of its creation, in union with the divine person of the Son of God. If the Son of God had taken to himself a man that had for some time previously existed, and that were already perfected, then it would of necessity

follow that there were in Christ two persons—the one assuming and the other assumed. But the Son of God did not assume a man that had previously existed. Or, in other words, the human nature was not first formed, and then united, after even the slightest interval of time, to the divine person; but it was formed and united by one and the same act, at one and the same moment: so that, while there are the two distinct natures, there is but the one divine person. And hence the infinite merit of all that Jesus did and suffered in our nature; it possessed all the worth and efficacy which his one divine person could attach to it. Oh, it was not merely that Jesus was the priest, but that he was also the sacrifice; it was not merely that he was the offerer, but that he was also the offering—it was this, in which the glory and efficacy of the sacrifice mainly lay. Hold fast, then, as you would hold eternal life, the simple Bible truth—Jesus the priest, but Jesus also the sacrifice. For rest assured of it, that the sacrifice of Christ will be to you just what the glory of his divine person makes it.

(2) But the second truth revealed to us here is *the voluntary character of all that Jesus did and suffered—the largeness and liberality of his love*. It is not said: 'I am sanctified,' as if he were merely passive; but 'I sanctify myself'—'I do it myself'—thus bringing out the voluntary character of all that he did. No wonder, therefore, that the good shepherd says of himself: 'No man taketh my life from me, but I lay it down of myself' (10:18). Oh! how wonderful is this love of Christ! Compulsion

did not bring him to the cross; persuasion did not induce him to undertake the work of our redemption; but his own love—love to his church, his bride—bore him on her soft wings from his throne in glory to the deepest abasement and suffering on earth. It was love—love to his church, his people—that moved him to veil his glory and appear in human form; it was love that led him through the whole course of his obedience and sufferings, and that brought him at last to Golgotha's fearful mount of doom. And so far as we are concerned, no other explanation can ever be given of it but free, unmerited, sovereign, boundless love: 'I sanctify myself.' I do it all myself.

Such, then, are the two great truths presented to us in these words—the mystery of Christ's person and work, and the mystery of his love.

And *the relation* in which this work stood to them is pointed out in the words, 'For their sakes'—not for his own sake, but for the sake of his disciples that were then upon the earth, and for all whom they represented to the end of the world. But this again is more fully explained in the words, 'That they also might be sanctified—consecrated—in truth.' The consecration of the disciples is here viewed as the *result* of the consecration of Christ. The whole self-sacrificing work of the disciples is traced up to the great sacrifice of Christ, as its cause, its origin. And the words: 'in truth' must here be taken, seeing the article is omitted, in the adverbial sense of—in a true manner—as opposed to the wholly outward consecration

of the Levitical priesthood. That they might be consecrated in *reality*—in the highest *spiritual* sense.

And indeed, if Jesus wholly set himself apart for his
people, *how reasonable, how befitting it is*, that they
should set themselves apart for him. Was he all for us
and shall we be nothing for him? Child of God, what
he was, he was for you; whatever he did, he did for you;
whatever he suffered, he suffered for you. Oh, then seek
to be all for him! Blessed exchange! Christ all for the
soul, and the soul all for Christ. 'Soul,' says the Saviour, 'whatever I am, I am for thee.' 'Saviour,' says the
soul, 'I am not worthy that thou shouldest accept of
me, but by thy grace, whatever I am, I am for thee.'

But if Christ consecrated himself wholly for their
sakes, *what a horrid evil must it be to 'count the blood
of the covenant an unholy thing'* (Heb. 10:29). And yet
I fear me, this is the very sin which is to be laid at the
door of some in my hearing. Oh, be very sure of this,
that if you know not how to estimate the merit of this
sacrifice, God does; he will make up the breaches which
you would make on the honour of his Son; he will draw
the pattern of your penalty from the heinousness of
your crime. And yet there is merit in the blood. 'Come
now, and let us reason together, saith the Lord: though
your sins be as scarlet, they shall be as snow; though
they be red as crimson, they shall be as wool.' 'And the
blood of Jesus Christ his Son cleanseth us from all sin.'

Christy Praying for the Entire Body of Believers—Spiritual Unity—Eternal Glory

John 17:20–24

HAVING prayed for himself as the *author* of our salvation, and for the apostles as the honoured *instruments*, in his blessed hand, in perpetuating and extending the knowledge of that salvation, Jesus proceeds next to pray for the entire body of believers, as those who were to be the *partakers* of his salvation to the end of the world. 'Neither for these alone do I pray, but for them also who shall believe on me through their word' (verse 20). Indeed, we have every reason to believe that when our Lord prays for the disciples he regards them not merely in their apostolic character—although this is certainly included—but also as *representatives* of all believers who may be placed in similar circumstances to the end of the world. But here he *explicitly assures* us that he is asking these things, not for the disciples only, but for them also who shall believe on him through their word: so that there is not a child of God now on the face of the earth, nor shall there ever be, but is included within the scope of this priestly prayer.

In describing the church of the future, Jesus assigns a most important place to the apostolic word: 'Who shall believe on me *through their word*.' He does not recognise here any other means, capable of bringing men to saving faith in him, except that of the divine word. And it is well for us to remember that the term rendered 'word' here denotes not merely the *narrative* of facts, or the *record* of the historical events; it includes also the *exposition* of these facts or events—the contents, in other words, of the Epistles, as well as of the Gospels. There is no *ordinary* means of coming to Christ—of saving faith in him—according to this passage, except that of the divine word. 'Faith cometh by hearing, and hearing by the word of God.'

But what does Jesus here pray for? What is the burden of his request for all believers? He prays for two things—*spiritual unity* (verse 21) and *eternal glory* (verses 22–24). These are the two all-comprehensive blessings which Jesus asks for the catholic church of believers.

[1] First, then, Jesus prays for *spiritual unity*: 'That they all may be one'; that is, that all believers may be one. And then having briefly indicated the general idea, he proceeds next to describe it as a union of the *highest order*—as sharing, in a manner, the nature of the union

between the Father and the Son: 'As thou Father art in me and I in thee, that they also may be one in us.' Deep and unfathomable words, easily said, but not so easily explained!

Observe, my friends, in attempting to get a little insight into their meaning, there is a *difference* here as well as a resemblance. He does not associate believers with *each* person of the Godhead, as he associates the persons of the Godhead with one another. He does *not* say that they are in the Father, *as the Son is in the Father*; or that they are in the Son, *as the Father is in the Son*. No, but he simply says: that they may be one in *us*—in us *both*. It is the union, in the first instance, of believers with the Father and the Son—with the Father through the Son—and so leading up, in the second place, to a real union of believers among themselves, and with one another.

And yet there must be a *resemblance* here; otherwise the comparison would never have been made. For just as the union between the Father and the Son is an *everlasting* one—can never be broken—so the union of believers with Christ, and in Christ with one another, can never be dissolved. As the union between the Father and the Son is *infinitely mysterious and unsearchable*, so is the spiritual tie which binds the souls of believers to God in Christ, and in Christ to one another, infinitely inscrutable and incomprehensible. 'The wind bloweth where it listeth, and thou hearest the sound thereof, but canst not tell whence it cometh, and whither it goeth: so is every one that is born of the Spirit.' And in a word, as that union between the Father and the Son is *ineffably glorious*, so also is this spiritual oneness of believers with Christ, and, in him, with one another.

And, moreover, it is plainly implied in these words that this union ought to be *visible*—tangibly expressed in holy deeds and words. For mark the *effect* that is here ascribed to it: 'that the world may believe that thou hast sent me.' It is very true, indeed, that there may be much of a *mere external, mechanical* union, that can never lead to such glorious results as are here specified: nay, but which rather operates in the very opposite direction—as is manifest in the case of the Church of Rome, and in that of other churches also that might be mentioned. But, on the other hand, it is perfectly clear that if the union of believers with one another is to be followed with the important consequences that are here ascribed to it, that union must be *expressed*; it must be *embodied in living words and actions.* Oh! brethren, it is not until the spiritual unity of believers in Christ shall show itself strong enough to destroy the selfishness, carnality, worldliness, and indifference that feed like a canker-worm at the root of our Christianity, in all the visible sections of it—it is not until then that we may expect the world to be won to the Saviour. It is when the Spirit shall be poured out upon us from on high, as the Spirit of truth and love, taking out of the way for ever sinful differences, jealousies, and heart-burnings;

producing astonishment, humiliation and shame, at past unfruitfulness and unprofitableness; drawing forth living, longing desires after a holy catholic union; and awakening deep yearnings of soul after a lost and perishing world—and all this manifesting itself in outward forms and palpable proofs—it is then, and only then, that we may expect the effect here announced to be produced; but then, it shall be produced without fail. Should not the churches of Christ, should not individual believers, ponder these things well? Should not the same mind be in us which was also in Christ Jesus, with reference to this matter? Should we not constantly pray that the day may speedily come, when, as there is but one shepherd, so there shall be but one sheepfold (10:16)?

Ah! yes, and never, perhaps, was the prayer more needed than in our own day. The church of God is *too much divided*. There is, indeed, a *real spiritual union* amongst all God's true people; let us thank God for that. But we cannot shut our eyes to the fact that there are too many divisions. Ephraim envies Judah, and Judah vexes Ephraim (Isa. 11:13). Sectarianism is one of the crying evils of the day, especially that sectarianism which works in the dark, and which affects great liberality, while carrying out its own sectarian ends. And what is the root of all this evil? Most undoubtedly one main source of it is *departure from the truth*. Truth is catholic; error is sectarian, and tends to divide. For there is such a thing as Christian principle, and the force of conscience. And he is the sectarian—not who adheres to fundamental truth and high Christian principle—but who deviates from the truth, and forsakes Christian principle. But whatever be the explanation of it, there can be no question that the present divided state of the visible church is a great obstacle to the furtherance of true religion. Let us earnestly pray that the Lord may bless his church with more unity; that he may take out of the way everything which divides her—every error which splits her up into fragments; that he may bring her to be one in the truth, one in Christ, and one in love to one another; that he may give her to know 'one Lord, one faith, one baptism.' So much, then, for the first blessing, which is here sought—spiritual unity.

[2] But from this subject our Lord rises now to *his last and highest request, even that they may become partakers with him in his glory.* Combining them into one united church—bearing upon his breastplate, before the Father, the entire body of believers—the great High Priest asks for them a share in his glory (verses 22–24).

And here you will observe that Jesus begins by declaring that the glory which the Father had given to him, he had given to them (verse 22). What then is the glory of which Jesus here speaks? What is this glory, which the Father had given him, and which he had given them? I know indeed that some interpreters, both ancient and modern, take no higher view of it than that of the apostolic office, and the power of working miracles. But certainly the words of Jesus take a loftier flight than this, as is manifest from verses 23 and 24. And besides, this view would confine the meaning to the apostles *only*, whereas it is distinctly referred by our Lord himself to believers of *all times* (verse 20). Others again, taking certainly a higher view of it, understand this glory of *the union*, of which he had just been speaking—compared, in a sense, to the glorious union between the Father and the Son. And I have no doubt whatever, from the words which immediately follow, that this is part, at least, of what is involved in it—the glory, in other words, of the indwelling Spirit. But to my mind these words, 'And the glory which thou hast given me I have given them' seem to stand in the closest possible relation to the words in verse 24, 'That they may behold my glory, which thou hast given me.' Oh, let us depend on it, it is not for nothing that *this statement* in verse 22, and *that prayer* in verse 24—*both referring to the glory which the Father has given to him*—are placed in such juxtaposition.

In attempting to ascertain the meaning of these wonderful words, 'And the glory which thou hast given me, I have given them,' it is well for us again to remember, what is a most beautiful and significant fact in itself, that *Jesus always, in this prayer, supports his petitions by mentioning what he himself had done towards the accomplishment of the end in view.* Thus, for example, does he pray: 'Holy Father, keep through thine own name those whom thou hast given me' (verse 11). Then he pleads: 'While I was with them in the world, I kept them in thy name' (verse 12). And again does he pray: 'Sanctify them through thy truth' (verse 17). Then he pleads: 'And for their sakes I sanctify myself that they also may be sanctified through the truth' (verse 19). And just so here, in proceeding to ask for them eternal glory, he lays a broad and solid foundation for his request, by declaring what he has himself already done for them. 'And the glory which thou hast given me I have given them.' 'I for my part, the glory which thou hast given me I have given them.' Let it also be distinctly borne in mind that *Jesus often speaks throughout this chapter, and indeed in these very words, as if he were already within the veil.* It is not said, 'And the glory which thou *shalt* give me,' but 'the glory which thou *gavest* me.' What then, I ask again, can this glory be of which Jesus here speaks? What, but the future glory of the heavenly kingdom, on which he was just about to enter, and in which all his people, in their measure, were to become sharers with him. And albeit they were not yet in *actual* possession of it, yet not the less on this account, was it theirs in the *right and title*. What the prayer in verse 24 asks is that *right* should be exchanged for *fact* and *full possession*. It is just as if he had said: 'And the glory which thou gavest me, I have given them in the right and title, ay, and in the earnest of it too.'

Taking this view of the subject, the words which follow may be regarded as setting forth *the purpose* which Jesus had in view: 'That they may be one, even as we are one.' But how can this be? How can believers be one as the Father and the Son are one? It is explained in the words which immediately follow: 'I in them, and thou in me' (verse 23). But God in Christ, and Christ in his people—what is this but the divine unity reproduced, in a manner, on earth! What is this but earth raised up to heaven! Then follows another result in close connection with this: 'that they may be perfected into one.' One in Christ Jesus—Christ Jesus in them all—they are to be perfected into one—*perfected*, but perfected into one; *into one*, but perfected into one; that is, compacted, consolidated into one glorious body.

And then follows another glorious result still: 'That the world may know that thou hast sent me, and hast loved them, as thou hast loved me.' Such is the wonderful character of this union, that, on beholding it, the world shall know assuredly the two following things: In the first place, it shall know that *the author of it— that he who has brought it about—is the sent one of God—the Father's commissioned servant.* And then, secondly, such shall be the beauties of holiness in which they, who are thus united, shall then shine, under the seal of the divine image, that it will then be perfectly manifest that they are *the objects of the same complacency and delight*, in their measure, as the Son himself. Glorious issue! Sublime consummation of the Saviour's work! No wonder that from this point he proceeds at once to speak of the ultimate design of all God's dealings with his church—even the direct contemplation and enjoyment of the glory of the Son of God. He has carried on, and followed up, his description of what he is to do for them and in them, until he has presented them as one body, perfect in 'the beauties of holiness.' Then comes the prayer: 'Father, I will,' etc. (verse 24). But on this department of the subject, we cannot for the present enter. Meanwhile, let us learn a few lessons from what has already been advanced.

And in the first place, do we not see here *the wonderful character of the union between Christ and his people*? Various are the similitudes under which it is represented to us in Scripture. It is compared to the union between the vine and the branches; to the union between the head and the other parts of the body; to that between the foundation-stone and the other parts of the building; and also to that between husband and wife—all most precious and significant emblems. But here, most wonderful of all, it is compared to the mysterious union between the Father and the Son. And while, of course, there is an infinite *difference*, there is also a *resemblance* between them.

And moreover, do we not see here that *the union of believers with Christ, and in Christ, with one another, is not a mere abstract principle, to be used only for the purposes of hair-splitting—not a mere dogma, to be written down in the creed of the churches, and then nothing more about it—but, on the contrary, a most vital, practical truth to be exemplified and embodied in life and action*? Far be it from us to advocate a mere external union, at the expense of the great fundamental truths of the gospel; nothing could be farther from our mind. But is it not truly lamentable to hear men sometimes magnify their own peculiar crotchets, which, of course, never had any place in the word of God, into important principles; and so rending asunder the body of Christ? Surely nothing could be more at variance with the prayer of the Saviour. Let us remember that, as in the days of his flesh, so *still* Jesus prays: 'That they all may be one'; and let us seek to realise that it is only as this prayer is answered—as answered it shall one day be—that it is only *then* that we have any reason to believe that the world shall be won to the Saviour.

Lastly, let us learn from this passage that *believers have even now in Christ Jesus a right and title to eternal glory.* Even now has he 'made them to sit together in heavenly places in Christ Jesus' (Eph. 2:6). The poorest believer on earth—though he were as poor as Lazarus lying at the rich man's gate, and desiring to be fed with the crumbs which fell from the rich man's table—is *a titled heir*—an heir of glory—a joint-heir with Christ; and soon he shall attain to his majority, and enter on the full enjoyment of his inheritance. With what earnestness, therefore, should each one of us enquire, 'Am I in Christ? Do I form one of the Christian brotherhood of which Jesus says: "I in them, and thou in me"?' There is safety, blessedness, glory only for those that are in Christ; but the apostle admits none to be in Christ except those, 'who walk not after the flesh, but after the Spirit' (Rom. 8:1).

Christ Praying for the Entire Body of Believers— Eternal Glory—Conclusion

John 17:24–26

I N the first of these verses, we have our Lord's last and highest request for his people, even that they may share with him in his glory. Having prepared the way for this, having laid a broad and solid foundation for it, by declaring what he himself had already done for them (verse 22), he comes now to utter it in these glorious words: 'Father, I will that they whom thou hast given me,' etc. The frequent use of the title 'Father,' at the close of this prayer (verses 21, 24, 25), reveals the increasing earnestness of Jesus, as he is drawing near to an end.

[1] Notice, in the first place, *the objects* of this prayer—the persons he is praying for. And that you may be enabled to see these the more clearly, it will be well to read the passage, as the words run literally thus: 'Father, that which thou hast given to me'—the

first thought here is of his people—'I will that where I am, there they also may be with me.' 'That which thou hast given to me' and 'they also'—these are the two clauses that express the *objects*. The neuter has a peculiar significance, *uniting*, as it does, *the whole church together as one gift of the Father to the Son* (6:39); it is the one body into which he had just said, 'they were perfected' (verse 23). While at the same time, the words, 'They also', *individualises*, *resolves* that body into its *individual* parts, and comes home to the heart of every believer, with the inexpressibly sweet assurance of an eternity with Christ.

But in what respects were this people given by the Father to the Son? In the first instance, he gave them to him *in the everlasting covenant*. When from all eternity he saw them lying in their guiltiness and sins, ready to perish for ever, he gave them to his Son to be by him in time redeemed, renewed, and brought home to glory. Ah! justly might he have left them to perish for ever in their sins, as he did the angels that fell, without any reflection on his justice, and without any disparagement of that goodness which had created them so holy and so happy, and which placed them in circumstances so favourable for securing and perpetuating that happiness. But no, to permit the whole human race to perish, when their covenant head had transgressed, did not seem good to him whose name is Love; but, on the contrary, in the exercise of his rich and sovereign grace, he gave a people to his Son to be by him redeemed and glorified, and to be to him the reward of his finished work.

But, in the second instance, the Father gives them to his Son *in the day of their espousals—in the day of their effectual calling.* 'All that the Father giveth me,' saith Jesus, 'shall come to me' (6:37)—not all that the Father gave me—as if he were speaking merely of some transaction in the past—but all that the Father *giveth* me—referring to the day of their espousals to Christ. And let us remember that it is as souls united to Christ, and effectually called in the day of the Spirit's power that our Lord regards them, when he here prays that they may be with him in glory. It is indeed true that Christ is here praying for the objects of his everlasting love; but it is also true that he does not pray that any may be with him in heaven, except those who are called, justified, and sanctified.

Do you remember Paul's golden chain in the eighth chapter of the Epistle to the Romans? 'For whom he did foreknow, them he also did predestinate' etc.; there is one link of the chain, and it stretches into the eternity that is past. But there are other links that appear in time: 'Whom he did predestinate, them he also called; and whom he called he justified.' While there is another link still that stretches into the eternity before us: 'Whom he justified, them he also glorified' (Rom. 8:29-30). It thus appears that, while there is one link in this golden chain that stretches back into the past eternity, and another that stretches forward into the eternity that lies before us, there are yet two intermediate and visible links upon which, if a man lay hold, he shall assuredly be saved—and these are effectual calling and justification. It is not essential to my salvation that I draw aside the veil, in the first instance, and read my name in the Lamb's book of life, and I may win to heaven with but a twilight glimpse of the coming glory. But I cannot get to heaven without the Spirit's grace and the Saviour's righteousness. Oh! grasp in faith, and receive into your heart, the two central and essential links—the Spirit's call and the Saviour's righteousness—and they will be to you evidences of God's eternal love to you, while, at the same time, they will carry after them eternal glory. 'Wherefore, brethren, give diligence to make your *calling* and election sure' (2 Pet. 1:10). It is for souls that are effectually called and justified that Jesus prays that they may be with him in glory.

[2] Notice, secondly, *the manner and spirit of this prayer.* Jesus no longer says 'I pray' (verses 9, 15, 20), but 'I will.' Oh, what a wonderful prayer is this! We never read of any prayer like this, offered up by any saint on earth. Some of them, indeed, attained to great nearness to the Lord—such as Abraham, and Jacob, and Moses, and David—and yet they never did, or ought to, use such language to God. Yea, we have nothing like this in all the accounts we have of Christ's own prayers at other times. We read of his spending whole nights in prayer; yet no such word was used by him. Oh, what a difference between it and his prayer

in his agony in the garden! The bitterness of the cup which was put into his hand, brought him to say: 'O my Father, if it be possible, let this cup pass from me.' But it was not possible, and therefore, in perfect resignation even as man to his Father's will, he says: 'Nevertheless not my will, but thine, be done.' But here it is: 'Father, I *will*.' Oh, see the difference between Christ's prayer when he is praying for himself in the hour of his agony, and when he is praying for eternal glory for his people! There it was: 'O my Father, if it be possible;' but here it is: 'Father, I will.'

And what shall we make of this prayer? I think we may say, in the first instance, there is in it *a beaming forth of his divine glory, as the eternal Son of God*. It is true, he was here in his state of humiliation; yet there were moments when scintillations of his divine glory did break forth, and we may well believe this to be one of them. And surely this expression sets forth *the reality and intensity of the Saviour's love*. It was in the exercise of infinite love that he laid down his life for them. 'I have a baptism to be baptised with, and how am I straitened till it be accomplished.' And it is in the exercise of the same love that he now intercedes for them. Further, we may well believe that this is an expression of will, *founded on acknowledged right*. Jesus had the price of our redemption now in his hand, ready to lay it down—the price fixed on in the everlasting covenant, the price of infinite value. And pleading on this foundation, need we wonder that he demands the blessing with this high word? 'Father, I will.' And, as has often been remarked, this *I will* on the part of Christ is *in perfect accord with the known will of his Father.* 'Father, I will,' says Christ; 'and I will too,' re-echoes the voice of the Father. Oh, blessed harmony this between the will of Christ and the will of his Father!

All this is most beautiful, most precious, and most interesting. But I apprehend that this unique expression—for it is a unique one, never used by the Saviour on any other occasion—is to be explained by *the unique character of the situation.* Jesus is just about to lay down his life for them, and he now expresses his last will and testimony: 'Father, my last will is.' It is truly his testimony which Jesus deposits in his Father's hands. We have an expression similar to this, when he says to his disciples: 'Peace I leave with you'—bequeath unto you—'my peace I give unto you.' Oh, blessed for evermore are they in whose behalf Jesus reads over his dying will in the ears of his Father!

[3] Let us now consider, thirdly, *what the blessings really are*, which Jesus thus asks for those that the Father gave him: 'That where I am, there they also may be with me, that they may behold my glory which thou hast given me,' etc.

First, he asks that *where he is, there they also may be with him.* Where was Jesus when he uttered this prayer? He was somewhere, we believe, on the slopes of Mount Olivet; and yet he prays as if he were already in glory: 'That where I am, they also may be with me.' Is not this the very thing which he had promised to the disciples: 'I will come again, and receive you unto myself, that where I am there ye may be also'? (14:3). Ah! yes, such is his love to them, that as he came from heaven to earth to save them, so he will never be at rest until he has them with him where he is. And is not this heaven—its chiefest, choicest ingredient—to be where Christ is? (Phil. 1:23). Oh, brethren, if communion with God on earth be so sweet, if the presence of God in means and ordinances be so precious, if one day in his courts is better than a thousand, what will an eternity in his immediate presence be?

But secondly, *why* does he pray that they may be with him where he is? How are they to be employed? Ah! they shall have work to do that shall never come to an end, and of which they shall never grow weary: 'That they may behold my glory which thou hast given me.' Deep words, but still deeper meaning!

Notice here *the object* to be beheld: 'My glory which thou hast given to me'—'My glory, peculiarly and emphatically—and yet, my glory which thou hast given to me'—not his essential glory as the Son of God viewed abstractly, and by itself; but the glory given to him as Immanuel, God-man, mediator. Oh, who can tell what glory now encircles him, as the Son of man exalted to the right hand of God! And yet this was what the Lord would have them to behold. Nay, he seems to pray for the one, because it leads to the other. We are not in a *condition* here fully to behold his glory. But

Jesus prays that they may be with him where he is, that they may behold it to full advantage.

But did they not behold this glory already? Assuredly they did by faith. And it is indeed a solemn truth, that none shall behold his glory by sight in heaven, that do not first behold it by faith on earth. Some beheld this glory before he came in the flesh (John 8:56; 12:41). Some beheld it by faith while he tabernacled upon earth (1:14). And some behold it now, though he is in heaven and they upon the earth. (2 Cor. 3:18). But the beholding mentioned in the text is something higher, nearer than all this. This is the *beatific vision* to which they shall attain when he has gathered them home to be for ever with himself. And if the vision on 'the holy mount' was so sweet, if the attractions of that moment were so ravishing that Peter said, 'It is good for us to be here,' what shall it be to behold the countless unfoldings of this glory throughout eternity? Indeed, it will be no mere vision, for we shall be like him, when we shall see him as he is (1 John 3:2). It is impossible to behold this glory, and to remain a mere spectator of it. To behold it is to *partake* of it—to become a *sharer* with him in his glory. Then shall be fulfilled the words: 'And the glory which thou gavest me I have given them.' This is the height to which Jesus elevates his church. Having raised his spouse from the mire, from the midst of a world immersed in evil, he introduces her into the sphere of his own glory, and places her down with himself upon his throne.

And one of the most interesting and delightful things connected with this glory, which they are to behold, will be to trace *the source of it in the Father's everlasting love*: 'The glory which thou hast given me, in that thou lovedst me.' I know indeed that many connect this last clause with the words: 'Father, I will,' as if Jesus were using the Father's love to him as his great plea in prayer. But I can see no good reason for separating the last clause from the words that immediately precede them; but very much the reverse: 'My glory which thou hast given me because thou lovedst me.' What wonderful love was this! The Father loved the Son with an everlasting love *as his Son*—his only begotten Son. But he also loved him with an everlasting love as *mediator*. 'Then I was by him as one brought up with him, and I was daily his delight' (Prov. 8:30). And it is just because of his love to him as mediator that he has put this crown of purest gold upon his head (John 10:17). Oh, surely it will be an eternal feast to the hearts of the redeemed in heaven to see the glorious unfoldings of the Father's love towards their covenant head.

Such, then, the two great blessings which Jesus here asks for the collective body of believers, namely, spiritual unity and eternal glory.

And now, in the last two verses of this chapter, our Lord concludes this whole prayer by a touching appeal in behalf of the disciples that were now before him. For this purpose, he lays hold of the righteous character of the Father; and just as before he appealed to the *holiness* of the divine character, when desiring the display of that perfection in preserving them from the contaminating influences of an evil world, so he now appeals to his *righteousness* or *justice*, when seeking to justify his petitions for them on the ground of their relation to himself: 'Oh righteous Father, the world hath not known thee, but I'—I who have placed myself at the head of these my people—'have known thee, and these have known me; and therefore, on the ground of the relation in which I stand to thee, and they stand to me, I appeal to thee in their behalf.' And what more does he say for them? 'And I have declared unto them thy name'—I who have known thee have made known unto them thy name. It is true indeed, it is yet but the twilight dawn in them, but I who have caused its first rays to shine upon them undertake to continue to reveal it: 'And will declare it.' How glorious the results at last! 'That the love wherewith thou hast loved me may be in them.' The Father loves the Son with a love of infinite complacency and delight, but so bright and beautiful will Jesus make them by the revelation of the Father that the same love of complacency shall rest on them as on him. Yea, so glorious will he make them at last that nothing will be seen in them but Christ. 'And I in them,' that is to say, Christ will be so truly living in them then, that nothing will be seen in them but his divine image.

Thus have I brought to a close what I had intended to say on this intercessory prayer, and with it also our exposition of this entire section of the Gospel narrative. And, slight and superficial as that exposition has been, what an amount of holy, heavenly truth has passed before our minds during these discussions! Jesus has compressed within these last moments the most sublime and spiritual lessons that were ever uttered upon earth. What calmness, what majesty too, what divine dignity, and yet what exquisite tenderness have prevailed throughout! Oh, surely if we were properly exercised, we could not rise from the perusal of these chapters without feeling that we have been in *the divine presence.*

I know indeed, that the question has been asked by rationalistic writers, 'How was John able to reproduce the words of his Master? Had he his writing materials in hand to take them down word for word?' And this is the way in which the oracles of the living God are treated by some who are appointed to be its expounders! But is there no account to be made of the promise of the Holy Spirit to guide into all truth? No, indeed, the inspired Evangelist had not writing materials in hand, we may well believe, nor did he need to have. No doubt the words of Jesus had graven themselves on the tablets of his loving heart; but over and above all this, he had the promise of the Spirit: 'But the Comforter, which is the Holy Ghost, whom the Father will send in my name, he shall teach you all things, and bring all things to your remembrance, whatsoever I have said unto you' (14:26).

What a blessed truth that the Saviour, who appears in these chapters, is still *the same*! Oh, brethren, if you would know what Jesus still is at the right hand of God, study him prayerfully as he is set before us in this precious portion of the evangelical narrative; think of him as stooping down to wash his disciples' feet; listen to the words of truth and consolation that proceeded from his blessed lips, and to the sublime intercessory prayer which he offered up to his Father in their behalf—and then clasp to your heart the truth that he, who thus acted and thus spake, is still the same: 'Jesus Christ, the same yesterday, today, and for ever.'

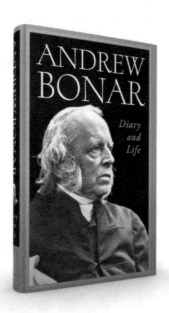

The Diary and Life of Andrew Bonar

Edited by Marjory Bonar

Andrew Bonar (1810–1892) belonged to the same school of Scottish Evangelicals as Charles Ross, and his diary provides a glimpse into the events and spiritual moods of a pivotal period in Scottish church history. He was a much-loved minister with a heart for evangelism, who moved from rural Perthshire to plant a new congregation in the working class area of Finnieston in Glasgow. His life was not without suffering, as his diary reveals, but as one who knew him well wrote, he 'seemed to live in a perpetual sunshine and to spread not gloom but brightness and good nature wherever he appeared.' His life-long concern was communion with God and his diary discloses that hidden yet most useful aspect of his witness. The 'Life' by his daughter adds detail to the diary's account.

ISBN 978 1 84871 183 9 | clothbound | 440 pages

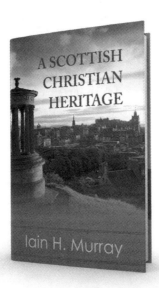

A Scottish Christian Heritage

Iain H. Murray

The compelling interest of this account lies in the way it draws on contemporary records—many of these Christian leaders being authors as well as men of action. Iain Murray's narrative explores this rich heritage and underlines its remarkable relevance for our own day. While not a Scottish church history, this is a gripping introduction to the many glorious successes, and some of the painful failures of the church, from the days of John Knox to those of Horatius Bonar. Explaining this panoramic tapestry are the words of Knox's own commentary, 'God gave his Holy Spirit to simple men in great abundance'.

As various recent publications have indicated, Scotland exercised an influence on world history out of all proportion to its size. But the real reason for this has been obscured. It will be found here, however. And in the discovery of it the reader will be introduced to a wealth of little-known literature that is a vital part of the inheritance of the whole Christian church.

— SINCLAIR B. FERGUSON

ISBN 978 0 85151 930 2 | clothbound | 416 pages

THE Banner of Truth Trust originated in 1957 in London. The founders believed that much of the best literature of historic Christianity had been allowed to fall into oblivion and that, under God, its recovery could well lead not only to a strengthening of the church, but to true revival.

Interdenominational in vision, this publishing work is now international, and our lists include a number of contemporary authors along with classics from the past. The translation of these books into many languages is encouraged.

A monthly magazine, *The Banner of Truth*, is also published. More information about this and all our publications can be found on our website or supplied by either of the offices below.

THE BANNER OF TRUTH TRUST

3 Murrayfield Road,
Edinburgh, EH12 6EL,
UK

PO Box 621, Carlisle,
Pennsylvania 17013,
USA

www.banneroftruth.org